KNOWING THE GOD YOU PRAY TO

Breakthrough Prayer Studies for Small Groups

CYNTHIA HYLE BEZEK

PRAYERSHOP PUBLISHING

Terre Haute, Indiana

PrayerShop Publishing is the publishing arm of Harvest Prayer Ministries and the Church Prayer Leaders Network. Harvest Prayer Ministries exists to transform lives through teaching prayer. Its online prayer store, www.prayershop.org, has more than 500 prayer resources available for purchase.

© 2015 by Cynthia Hyle Bezek

All rights reserved. No part of this publication may be reproduced in any form without written permission from PrayerShop Publishing, P.O. Box 10667, Terre Haute, IN 47801.

ISBN: 978-1-935012-56-6

Some of the anecdotal illustrations in this book are true to life and are included with the permission of the persons involved. All other illustrations are composites of real situations, and any resemblance to people living or dead is coincidental.

Unless otherwise identified, all Scripture quotations in this publication are taken from the *Holy Bible, New International Version*® (NIV®). Copyright © 1973, 1978, 1984 by International Bible Society. Used by permission of Zondervan. All rights reserved.

Other versions used include: the *Holy Bible*, New Living Translation (NLT), copyright © 1996, 2004. Used by permission of Tyndale House Publishers, Inc., Carol Stream, Illinois 60188. All rights reserved; *THE MESSAGE* (MSG). Copyright © 1993, 1994, 1995, 1996, 2000, 2001, 2002. Used by permission of NavPress Publishing Group; the *Amplified Bible* (AMP), © The Lockman Foundation 1954, 1958, 1962, 1964, 1965, 1987; and the New King James Version (NKJV). Copyright © 1982 by Thomas Nelson, Inc. Used by permission. All rights reserved.

Printed in the United States of America

1 2 3 4 5 | 19 18 17 16 15

Table of Contents

Introduction

THIS STUDY IS ABOUT getting to know the God we pray to. I mean *really* knowing Him.

I grew up in the church, so I figured I knew God. After all, I logged hours and hours learning about Him in Sunday school, Sunday morning and evening services, youth group, Wednesday-night prayer meetings, Vacation Bible School, church camp, Bible quiz meets, revival meetings, missionary conferences—how could I *not* know God?

Yet my prayers were pretty impersonal. I asked God to meet needs, and I confessed sin and asked for help to obey. I prayed mostly because good Christians are supposed to do it, not because I enjoyed relating with God.

Over time, God stirred a holy discontent in me. I was no longer satisfied with a cordial but distant relationship with Him. I realized I had only a narrow understanding of Him, which skewed my perceptions of what He was like. As I invited God to reveal Himself to me more fully, I started enjoying Him like never before and my prayers took on new life.

In this study, I will share some of the basic truths I learned on my journey to knowing God, such as:

- God longs to be known and delights in our seeking to know Him.
- Knowing God means experiencing a meaningful relationship with Him, not accruing information about Him.

- We all suffer to some extent from an incomplete or distorted knowing of God. The more completely and accurately we know Him, the more we will want to talk with Him.
- God reveals many facets of Himself in Scripture; each one gives us a different way to relate to and talk with Him.

Recognizing there is a whole lot more to God than I ever knew has transformed the way I pray, and I hope it does the same for you. Before we begin that transformation, I want you to know some foundations this study is built on.

First, the study assumes that prayer—at its most basic level—is a relationship with God and that God Himself is very relational. That's why, in the pages ahead, we'll talk so much about relationship and about communicating with God as a real Person.

Also, prayer is a two-way interaction. When you pray, you're not submitting a request to a distant deity who may or may not get back to you; you're talking with a very present God who has committed Himself to live life with you 24/7. You'll be encouraged to talk with God and then be quiet and listen to what He wants to say to you in reply.

Finally, because prayer is two-way relational conversation, it can happen in a variety of formats. We'll talk about many different modes of praying so you can enjoy new ways of talking with God. Although some of these modes may be new, I encourage you to involve yourself—your whole self—in the ways the lessons invite you to. If you're asked to pray, please take time to pray. If you're asked how you feel about something, please search your heart and try to discover that. If you're asked to be honest about your experiences with God, please be honest, even if you have been disappointed or confused.

It takes time, openness, and a certain degree of emotional risk to get to know our glorious God intimately, but I guarantee that it's worth the effort!

How to Get the Most from This Study

THIS STUDY IS DESIGNED to provide practical, hands-on opportunities for you to grow deeper in your relationship with God through prayer. With that in mind, realize that you will get the most out of the study if you do each lesson on your own and come to your group time prepared to share what you have experienced and where you may be struggling.

During the week, you'll explore how God has revealed Himself through Scripture and you'll interact with Him through prayer. As a guideline, plan to spend twenty to thirty minutes a day in the lesson. You will be asked to read Scripture, reflect, respond, and try out what you learn in prayer practice. The format of your assignments could make an ideal devotional time, if you'd like to think of it that way. Spending time on your lesson every day saves you last-minute frustration and, more important, reinforces a pattern of relating personally to God daily.

Each lesson in this study moves through the following rhythm: (1) "Open Up to God," which includes a simple prayer you can pray at the beginning of each lesson to make yourself available to God and to invite Him to do the lesson with you; (2) "Discover Who God Is," a section of questions that introduces the key concepts for each lesson and asks you to interact with Bible passages; (3) "Respond to God," which provides prayer exercises that will help you talk with God about what you've discovered in the thought and study questions; and (4) "Continue the Conversation," a closing to the lesson with suggestions for how to incorporate the week's prayer focus into everyday life.

How you divide up a lesson over a week is up to you. I'll give suggestions for how you can proportion the lessons, but feel free to work through them in the manner that works best for you. Just keep one important factor in mind: Pace yourself so you allow several days for prayer. Because the object of this study is not to learn *about* prayer but actually *to pray*, the prayer exercises are essential. If you only work through the questions and participate in group discussion, you will miss the whole point of the study. So when the lesson prompts you to talk with God about something, *please talk with God.* You learn to pray by praying.

As you answer questions, discuss, and pray, you may notice this study is different from others you have done and it might require a different approach from you. Many studies are aimed at gaining information about the Bible or a spiritual topic. This one focuses on transforming how you relate with God. I encourage you to enter into an experiential, discovery mode. Instead of just "trying to get homework done" or "reading passages to fill in the blanks with the right answer," let these lessons guide you into real, relational conversations with God.

Relational transformation will happen if you are willing to adopt several important approaches:

- Be honest with yourself and God about where you are in your relationship with Him and how you feel about talking with Him. Prayer is a vulnerable topic for many people, even pastors and spiritual leaders. Many of us (maybe even most of us) are not where we want to be when it comes to prayer. If you are willing to be honest about your disappointments and struggles, this study can move you closer to where you hope to be.

- Be willing to be stretched. Some of the questions and exercises will move you out of your comfort zone. Please enter in, even if you are doubtful or unsure. Others who have done this study reported that if they were willing to try the prayer responses, they were surprised at how God met them and how talking with Him became more rewarding.
- Respect where you are—and where others in your group are—on your journey with God in prayer. Don't be afraid to share your struggles and disappointments with other members. At the same time, be sensitive when other members share their weaknesses. Don't try to coach them with what works for you; let the Holy Spirit do that. Accept others where they are right now. Help create a safe environment for everyone to be vulnerable.

What I will share with you in this study only begins to scratch the surface of how you can relate with God, but that's okay. My goal is to ignite in you a passion to know and relate to our amazing, infinite God!

Note to Group Leaders: A leader's guide can be downloaded at www.harvestprayer.com/resources/free-downloads. You'll find detailed information in the guide for how to begin and facilitate this study.

Knowing God

Suggestions for Pacing the Lesson

Days 1–3: Work through the "Discover Who God Is" questions and do the first "Respond to God" prayer exercise.

Days 4–7: Do the second prayer-response exercise and move on to the "Continue the Conversation" suggestion.

1. Who are you? Complete three of the following prompts:

I highly value . . . *family + friends.*

I've worked as an . . . *office assistant*

I enjoy talking about . . .

I like to . . .

I'm good at . . . *decorating + hospitality + listening.*

Someday I'd like to . . .

CYNTHIA'S STORY

When I moved to Colorado a number of years ago, my husband was seriously ill with a progressive illness. People we didn't know soon recognized us because of my husband's wheelchair and obvious handicaps, and they would often strike up conversations about those things. How was David feeling that day? Who were his doctors? Had we tried certain drugs and nutritional supplements? How was I managing with the demands of caregiving? Did we know about the multiple sclerosis support group? Had we read a particular book on divine healing? Did we know so-and-so who also had an incurable neurological disorder?

In the other cities where we had lived, people knew my family based on our personalities, activities, interests, and passions. They knew I played the violin and wrote articles and liked hanging out with international people. They knew I was intense and hospitable and loved a great conversation about big ideas. They knew that my husband was a computer engineer, percussionist, and inventor and a really nice guy with a gentle disposition and a dry sense of humor. And they knew that our son loved to read about Persia and talk about weather, the stock market, and sports.

We got lots of attention in our new community, but it was narrowly focused. I felt as though no one really knew me. Instead of being an interesting person in my own right, I seemed to be the Wife of the Man in the Wheelchair. I longed for someone to take time to know and understand me.

2. Just as we may know people in only one or two ways, we may inad-

vertently limit ourselves to knowing God through only one or two of His facets. Try an experiment that may stretch you a little. Following are the same prompts you answered before. This time, answer them as if God were the one answering. What does God highly value? What work has He done? What does He enjoy talking about?

I [God] highly value . . . *Spending time with My children.*

I've worked as a . . . *Carpenter*

I enjoy talking about . . . *What's on your heart.*

I like to . . . *hear our praises*

I'm good at . . .

Someday I'd like to . . .

How did it go? It was probably somewhat difficult because the prompts took you outside the norms of how we usually think about God. You may even have wondered if it's okay to talk about God in those categories. But just as I wanted to be known as more than the Wife of the Man in the Wheelchair, God wants to be explored and known more fully.

In this lesson, you'll discover how knowing God more fully and accurately can greatly expand and enrich the way you pray, relate to, and enjoy Him. My goal is to launch you on a lifetime treasure hunt of knowing God and exploring His many facets!

OPEN UP TO GOD

3. We want to start each lesson by acknowledging that God is with us as we study Him. So in this "Open Up to God" section at the start of each lesson, I'll encourage you to invite God to do the lesson with you. You may borrow this prayer or use your own words:

> God, I hardly know what to expect as I begin this new study. But I do want to know You better, and I do want a deeper relationship with You. So will You please help me as I read and pray? I'll be drawing near to You. Will You please draw near to me?

DISCOVER WHO GOD IS

As you'll soon see, God wants to be discovered! He wants to be known for who He really is, as a real Person with real thoughts, desires, and emotions. In this "Discover Who God Is" section, you will be asked to look up scriptures and think about and respond to them. Try to do this in a relational, heart-soul-mind-and-strength way. Your goal is to see God as He really is so you can engage with Him personally.

4. Many of us haven't given much thought to how our relationship with God—or lack of it—affects *Him*. God repeatedly confided to Jeremiah the prophet His desire to be known. Read Jeremiah 2:8, 4:22, 9:23-24, 24:7, and 31:34.

a. What stands out to you from these verses about knowing God?

God truly wants us to know Him

b. How is knowing information about God different from knowing *Him?* The same as the difference between being acquainted w/someone + having a relationship w/someone I can be acquainted & not know their

c. Why do you think God wants to be known? What's in it for heart Him? He wants that intimacy with us, He longs for that.

d. What benefits might there be for you if you were to get to know Him as He wants to be known? We would be more in tune w/Him. I think we'd follow His direction better if we knew Him better. We would trust Him more.

HOW WE KNOW GOD AFFECTS HOW WE PRAY

The more we know about another person, the greater the foundation we have for conversation. The same is true for God. By the end of the study, you'll know more things that He's good at, more of what He likes to do, and more words to describe Him. You'll be talking with Him differently as you pray.

5. Describe how you ordinarily perceive God as you pray. For example, by what name or title do you usually address Him (God, Lord, Jesus, and so on)? Do you tend to picture Him in any particular way (on a throne, on the cross)? For what attributes do you typically praise Him? Don't over-think this—just note how you *usually* think of God when you pray.

He walked + talked + lived among us.

I call him Lord. Honestly I think of Him as a high being. High above me. But He came to earth as a human to walk + talk among us. Why would I see Him like that?

6. What is something you often pray about on an ordinary day (for example, something going on in your children's lives, a ministry you're in at church, a situation you read about in the news)?

7. Now that you have in mind how your prayers ordinarily sound, practice praying differently. Instead of addressing God as you normally would, talk to Him according to a facet of His character. Choose two of the following three prayer starters to form the beginning of a one-sentence prayer about the prayer topic you listed in question 6.

"Yaweh, my Strong Tower, I know You are a place of refuge. I would like to talk with You about . . ."

"Jesus, my Bridegroom, I know that You love me intensely as Your bride, and I would like to talk with You about . . ."

"Holy Spirit, my Comforter, I know that You want to come alongside me in all that troubles me. I would like to talk with You about . . ."

8. How did addressing God according to these (thoroughly biblical) roles affect the way you prayed?

9. What we perceive about God changes the way we address Him and what we talk to Him about. Likely, most of us are more comfortable with some of His characteristics than others. Consider the following true statements about God:

- God is Creator and Sustainer of all that is, overseeing galaxies and natural disasters, nations and kingdoms, and unseen spiritual realms in heaven, on earth, and under the earth.
- God is love, grace, and mercy and does not delight in punishing people.
- God is Judge and Ruler over every living creature, with full authority to govern and reign.
- God is a miracle worker who raises the dead, heals the incurable, parts the seas, turns water into wine, stops the sun, and feeds multitudes from a single lunch sack.

Does one of those descriptions of God resonate more with you than the others? Which one?

10. If the statement you chose was the only truth you knew about God, how might your perception of Him be limited or even distorted by what you did not know about Him?

Just now, I read the above list of God's characteristics to my twentysomething son so we could talk them over. I felt a bit exposed when, after hearing the description of God as Judge and Ruler, he interjected, "That's the one you really believed, isn't it?"

He was right. For many years, that was my dominant view of God. This viewpoint was biblically sound and led me to a high view of God. However, focusing on this one aspect of God's character also led me to a distortion that constantly affected the way I lived, felt about Him, and related to both Him and others. My son went on to describe how he had observed this belief affecting me: "You believed that God was always out to make sure you got everything right and was just waiting to punish you when you didn't."

That is how I reacted to God. I felt as if I were constantly on trial before my Judge and had to work hard every day to measure up. I desperately needed my view of Him as Ruler and Judge to be balanced by an equally accurate view of His love, grace, and mercy. When God started revealing those aspects of Himself to me, I was gradually able to relax and enjoy Him more. I began to talk to Him in new ways.

Instead of prayers dominated by concerns about performance ("Help me obey" or "Help me please You" or "Forgive me for messing up"), I could now begin connecting with God as a loving Father and Friend who enjoyed me, invited me to take risks, redeemed my mistakes, and understood my weaknesses. Gradually my prayers became more open and vulnerable. ("Father, I am struggling to love this person—will You help me understand what's really going on inside me?" "Jesus, I'm afraid. I want to trust You, but this circumstance is really making me anxious. Please help me rest in Your love and see Your grace for me.")

What's been especially surprising and encouraging is that when I relate to God in these new ways, I sense His pleasure. He is glad I am relating to Him with a bigger, richer, more accurate picture of who He is. I hear Him saying, "Child, I longed to touch your heart, but I couldn't when you focused solely on getting everything right because you were fearful of being punished. I love being able to simply love you and pour out My grace and mercy into your everyday life."

Can you relate with my experiences? Is a one-sided view of God affecting how you relate with Him? I hope that, through this study, you'll begin to find new freedom and depth with Him.

RESPOND TO GOD

In this section, I'll give you hands-on ways to respond personally to God. After all, this study is about prayer, so we want to actually talk and relate with God about all the things we're discovering about Him.

PRAYER RESPONSE 1: Knowing God

a. Read the following statements. Which ones express your thoughts and feelings? Put a check mark by as many as you identify with (even if they seem contradictory).

_____ I know God pretty well, but not as well as I want to. Bring it on!

_____ If I get to know God better, He'll probably demand more from me. I don't know if I'm up for that.

_____ I already know that God is big, powerful, and in charge. Do I need to know more? I don't want to diminish Him.

_____ If I get to know God better, will He want to know me better too? I'm not sure I want to get that close to "fire."

_____ I have to be honest: God seems pretty vague and amorphous to me. How do you get to know a Spirit? Is it really possible to relate to Him as you would a flesh-and-blood person?

_____ I like some things about God's character but other things not as much. Can I just stick to the parts about Him that I like?

_____ I've heard lots of good press about God, but my experience with Him doesn't match up.

_____ I have lots of questions about God. I'd like a chance to get them answered.

_____ I know a lot *about* God, but I'm not so sure I *know* God.

_____ It's not just God I have a hard time connecting with—it's people in general. I just don't think I'm very relational.

_____ Other:

b. Look over the statements you checked. Choose one to form the basis of a conversation with God.

(1) Use the statement as a starting place to write a prayer to God. Don't worry that He might not like what you have to say. He already knows your thoughts and feelings, and He desires truth in the innermost part of your being (see Psalm 51:6). Your honesty pleases Him and is a great first step toward getting to know Him better. The following questions and ideas may help you flesh out what you want to talk to Him about.

- Are you content with what this statement or question says about your thoughts and feelings about God? Why or why not?

- If you're uneasy about the statement you identified with, do you know where the thoughts or feelings it expresses originated? Were you perhaps taught it somewhere, whether overtly or subtly?

- What risk do you run if you invite God to reveal more of Himself to you? Are you ready to take that risk? Why or why not?

- Is it possible that what you think or feel about God is inaccurate or incomplete? If so, how could you open up to letting God reveal Himself more accurately and completely?

- Do any of the things you feel or believe about God seem contradictory? Would you like to tell God about that and invite

Him to bring clarity?

(2) After you have expressed yourself to God, sit quietly and listen for Him. How do you sense Him responding to what you shared? If you're uncertain of what God's response might be like, here are some ways He sometimes speaks:

- You might feel or sense something. For instance, do you sense He is pleased with your coming to Him like this? Or do you feel a sense of peace deep inside?
- Perhaps a song started playing in your head or a Scripture passage came to mind.
- Maybe you "saw" a picture of something that brought comfort or insight.
- Sometimes a thought or phrase will come to you; this can be God's Holy Spirit communicating with you.

Write down what you sense God saying.

Example. Here is an example of what this prayer exercise might be like. First, I write out my prayer to God:

I've heard lots of good press about You, God. Your Word describes You as good and loving, always present, always protecting and providing and caring. But I have to be honest: My experience with You doesn't always match up. You've allowed a lot of pain and loss in my life, and I'm a bit afraid of when the other shoe is going to drop.

I feel guilty for doubting Your goodness and kindness; it's hard for me to "know you" in those ways. I want to believe those things about You, and part of me actually does believe them. But my heart is slow. I have so many questions. If You love me so much, why have You allowed so much hardship?

After waiting for a few minutes in silence, I sense how God might be responding to me and write it down:

God might be saying that any answer He gives to my "Why?" questions would fail to satisfy me. He reminds me that His ways are higher than mine and it's hard for me to recognize His goodness from my limited vantage point. I sense Him telling me that I'm not looking for explanations as much as reassurance of His love and faithful presence and that He really is always working things together for my good.

I want to continue my conversation with God, so I ask Him a different question:

Father, will You be with me now? Will you pour Your love into my heart and set my heart at rest in Your presence? Will you help me to be open to getting to know you better even though I don't understand?

Then I wait silently again before I note what I'm experiencing:

I do feel more peaceful—not like everything is answered or solved, but like He is with me and will help me, probably over

*days and weeks and months, to be able to experience His love
more deeply. Maybe really getting to know Him isn't going to be
as full of as much doubt and struggle as I'd thought it would be.*

Start your own conversation with God and make notes here:

PRAYER RESPONSE 2: Talking with God according to a Name or Title

Ask God to reveal one of His names or titles He would like you to focus on so you can talk to Him in fresh ways.

a. One way God might reveal a name or title to focus on is through His
Word. If you are in the habit of reading the Bible every day, ask Him to
reveal the aspect of Himself He'd like you to discover as you read that
day. (If you need some passages to begin with, consider these as possibilities: Psalm 91; Isaiah 61; Matthew 6:25-34; John 15:1-8; Revelation 5.)

You could also ask God to speak to your heart about an aspect of
Himself that He wants to reveal to you. Then listen quietly and pay attention to what crosses your mind. Do you see a picture, hear a Scripture passage, have an impression, or hear a specific word or phrase?
Talk to Him about what He seems to be telling you.

b. Whichever means He uses to reveal Himself to you, consider that
name or title and then write down something for each of these categories:

A way to picture Him according to this name or title:

Attributes for which you can praise Him according to this name or title:

Topics or issues you can pray about according to this name or title:

Example. Here is an example of what this prayer response looked like for me.

Today I read Job 1, where Satan and the other angels present themselves before God, and Satan and God discuss God's servant, Job. As I let the passage roll around in my heart and mind, I pictured this fallen angel appearing before the Lord, along with the rest of the angelic hosts. What a mighty God I had, to command and rule in such a scene! I thought of various pictures and names for God that I'd encountered elsewhere in Scripture. I recalled that one of His names is "Lord of hosts." I remembered that somewhere (turns out to be Joshua 5:15) He's also addressed as "commander of the Lord's army." As I continued to meditate prayerfully on passages the Holy Spirit brought to mind, here's how I filled in my prayer prompts:

- Name or title by which I can address God:
  Lord of hosts, commander of the Lord's army
- Way to picture Him according to this name or title:
  I see God on His throne, ruler of everyone and everything that is brought before Him.
- Attributes for which I can praise Him according to this name or title:
  He is powerful; sovereign over all creation; victor over evil, sin, and death; greater than the one who is in the world; He has all authority and is the final word.
- Topics I can pray about according to this name or title:
  A ministry couple I know are in a time of intense spiritual

*testing; Israel is in the news again and the world is taking
sides; my church faces serious struggles because of financial
shortfalls, loss of staff, and the pastor's health issues.*

c. Then pray to God according to that name or title.

> **Example.** *Ordinarily, my prayer for one of the topics I listed
> might sound like this: "Lord, give this couple grace and strength
> to come through this testing in a way that is good for them and
> brings glory to You."*
>
> *But today, because I was praying according to God's role as
> Lord of hosts, I prayed, "Lord of hosts, You know what is going on
> behind the scenes in this trial my friends face. Please expose Sa-
> tan's lies and strategies. Please silence his harassment and halt his
> schemes. Show Yourself victorious on behalf of my friends, Your
> son and daughter, in this malicious spiritual attack."*

Do you see how relating to God in ways beyond "Lord" and "Father in heaven" can expand your prayers? Here's an outline you can use
to walk you through your conversation with God:

- Name or title by which I can address God:
- A way to picture Him according to this name or title:
- Attributes for which I can praise Him according to this name
  or title:
- Topics or issues I can pray about according to this name or title:

Write the first few sentences of your prayer to God, according to
this name or title:

CONTINUE THE CONVERSATION

The more we practice and put into action what we've learned, the more it makes a difference in our lives. We'll finish each lesson by continuing to relate to God in prayer during the days until your group meets for discussion. I know that real life often makes it hard to sit down and talk with God regularly, but in my experience, the rewards for getting to know God more fully have more than paid for the time I've invested.

In the days before your next group meeting, continue to use Prayer Response 2. You might keep on praying according to the name or title God showed you, or you might ask Him for a different name or title each day.

Write your prayer notes here or in a journal.

Our Good Shepherd

FEEL FREE TO WORK through the lesson at your own pace, breaking it up over several days if you'd like. Just remember that the key to this study is prayer, so be sure to leave time for the prayer portions. Set appointments with yourself on your calendar if that would be helpful.

This lesson includes a summary of prayer starters at the end; you can start using this during the week if you'd like.

Suggestions for Pacing the Lesson

Days 1–3: Work through the "Discover Who God Is" questions.
Days 4–5: Do the "Respond to God" prayer exercises.
Days 6–7: Use the "Continue the Conversation" suggestions.

CYNTHIA'S STORY

I think sheep are kind of endearing. To me, they have sweet, innocent faces and seem to live carefree lives, frolicking around the pasture, enjoying themselves.

But my friend who grew up on a Midwestern sheep farm suggests that my view is naïve and romanticized. In her experience, sheep are vulnerable, stubborn, and stupid. They are not carefree—actually, they are in constant danger of death. She says there is no limit to the ways they find to get themselves killed. They follow each other, blind-leading-the-blind, into all manner of mortal peril. They drown themselves in shallow creeks. They wander off and fall into holes or get caught in bushes or get eaten by coyotes. They get their heads stuck in fences, and if someone doesn't notice and rescue them, they die. In the winter when they eat grain instead of grass, you have to watch them because they don't know when they're full and will eat themselves to death.

They're dirty, smelly, and obstinate, she says. They startle easily. They can't do anything for themselves, but when you try to help them, they run away from you. My friend wouldn't dream of picking one up and carrying it on her shoulders or next to her chest. "It would probably kick me in the head with its hard little hooves!"

"So is there anything good about sheep?" I wondered aloud. "I mean, why would anyone ever want to be a shepherd?" Her sardonic reply: "Sheep don't smell as bad as pigs."

As I pondered what my friend said—how unattractive and difficult sheep can be, how utterly needy yet resistant to help—I began to appreciate how good the Good Shepherd truly is.

In the previous lesson, we saw how much God desires us to know Him fully and relate to Him for all of who He is. In this lesson and the ones that follow, we're going to practice doing just that. We'll study and relate with God according to one aspect of His character. This time we'll focus on Him as our Good Shepherd.

OPEN UP TO GOD

1. Let's start by talking to God. Invite God, the Shepherd, to teach you about Himself. You may borrow this prayer or use your own words:

> God, I choose to set aside some time to get to know You
> better. Please help me focus on You and not be distracted
> by all the stuff in my life. Open my heart to see, know,

and relate to You in new ways. Would You help both You
and me to really enjoy this time together?

DISCOVER WHO GOD IS

Think of this section as an opportunity to find something new about
God for the purpose of relating with Him.

Suppose I wanted to introduce you to one of my friends. I might
say, "Meet Bill. He's one of the funniest guys I know. He has a wealth
of practical wisdom and a huge heart. He risked his life once to save
mine. And even though that's a cool story, I really want you to meet
him because you two have a ton in common. You both love middle
schoolers and find ways to bring out their potential. And you've both
had rough experiences with loss. I think you and Bill are going to enjoy each other."

Imagine that you jot notes during this inspiring introduction:
"Good sense of humor. Practical. Loving. Lifesaver, risk-taker. Loves
middle schoolers. Grew through loss." You then put the notes in your
pocket and walk away, leaving Bill and me just standing there. If that
happened, my introduction would have failed, and both you and Bill
would have missed an opportunity for a great friendship.

Of course, you'd never just walk away like that, yet for a long time I
did something similar with Bible study. I'd take copious notes about God
and then tuck them away and walk off without engaging with Him.

I hope for better things for you! I hope learning these various aspects of God will lead you to engage with Him. I want you to enjoy
Him at altogether new levels and in more relational, satisfying, life-
giving ways.

2. We'll start by exploring what Scripture reveals about God as our
Shepherd. The following passages are some of the key places in the

Bible where God uses the Shepherd/sheep picture.

Read each passage and make notes about the ways shepherds care for their sheep. Continue asking for God's help in getting to know Him: "Shepherd, please help me see You as You really are so I can relate to You more personally and fully."

a. 1 Samuel 17:34-35

b. Psalm 23

c. Psalm 78:52-53

d. Isaiah 40:11

e. Ezekiel 34:11-16

f. Luke 15:3-7

g. John 10:1-17, 25-27

3. As you read about how shepherds care for sheep, what—if anything—did you notice the sheep doing for the shepherd?

4. How different might your prayers be if sometimes you related to God as Shepherd instead of Lord and Master?

5. Now, keeping in mind the information about God that you discovered in question 2, use the next pages to revisit and sink into the three passages that impressed you most. This is where we're departing a little from a normal Bible study routine so we can interact with what we are learning more personally. Remember, the goal isn't to scan a verse for the right answer, note it, and move on; it's to get to know God. That's why it's worthwhile to let each passage roll around in your heart and mind for a while. You might try reading the scripture out of a Bible version you don't regularly use so the language is fresh to you.

As you consider the passage, pay attention to ideas that intrigue you, questions you might like to ask God about His role as our Shepherd, your own experiences that dovetail with the passage, feelings (positive or negative) you have about Him, images or pictures that come to mind, songs or poems that remind you of who He is, and so on.

Use the space to jot notes, doodle key words, draw pictures, or capture your thoughts in whatever ways work best for you and God. Employ both your mind and your heart and have fun. (I can hear some of you protesting, "But I'm not creative!" or "I can't draw!" No problem. I'm just inviting you to think outside the box of "I have to look up a verse and create a list of key points" and be yourself with God.)

Example: Isaiah 40:11

Jesus, I love the idea of Your holding me close to You. I think I'd like to be there for a few minutes right now. I feel safe here, Jesus. Even though I'm grown up, it's really good to know I can be a little kid sometimes and have You care for me like this, so gently and tenderly. Help me to come to You like this when I am overwhelmed or afraid or upset.

1 Samuel 17:34-35

Psalm 23

Psalm 78:52-53

Isaiah 40:11

Ezekiel 34:11-16

Luke 15:3-7

John 10:1-17,25-27

6. One of the fascinating things about the Shepherd picture is that several times God contrasts bad shepherding and how He takes care of His sheep. Read the following Scripture passages: Ezekiel 34:1-10; Jeremiah 50:6-7; Matthew 9:36; John 10:1-13. What happens to sheep who have poor shepherding or none at all?

Reflections about good and bad shepherding:

7. Based on the verses you reflected on in questions 2 and 6, describe your Shepherd. Imagine you are introducing Him to another "sheep." What does your Shepherd want for you? How does He want sheep to be treated? How does He want them to feel? (Pray, "God, will You reveal Yourself to me as a Shepherd? What do You especially want me to notice about Yourself? How do you want to be known?")

   God, our Good Shepherd, is . . .

8. Does what God has shown you highlight any misconceptions you may have held about Him? For example:

- Some people who have come to believe they must take care of themselves avoid the Shepherd picture, thinking only "weak" people need a pretty picture of a Shepherd or that only people with extreme needs qualify for His care.
- Bad shepherding from pastors or spiritual leaders may cause people to be bitter, angry, or blaming toward God.
- The Shepherd's rod may cause some people (especially ones who were abused or punished harshly as children) to fear coming close to Him.

- Some people may resent that the Shepherd would leave the ninety-nine "good" sheep to go after the one wayward sheep.

How might you counteract these misconceptions based on what God is revealing about Himself to you? Invite His help: "Shepherd, will You help me see You clearly and see myself clearly? I want to relate to You as You truly are, not as I perceive You to be."

A misconception I'm prone to about God:	*How His Good Shepherd picture counteracts that misconception:*

CYNTHIA'S DISCOVERIES ABOUT HER GOOD SHEPHERD

As I interacted with God about what it meant that He was a good shepherd, two themes really struck me and changed the way I prayed.

First, I was struck by how He is the one taking responsibility for the sheep, serving them, and caring for them. When I used to think about my relationship with God, I thought about what He required from me, what He deserved, and how well I was meeting those expectations—and of course, He is absolutely worthy of my obedience and service. But when my relationship with God and prayer life focused primarily on working for and obeying Him, He didn't get to shepherd me much. The way I saw it, servants serve their masters, not the other way around, so I'd shepherd myself, thank you very much.

It took me a long time to see the twist in my thinking. Eventually, I saw that even though my approach might appear humble and

God-honoring, it really was neither. My focus was more on me than on God. I was preoccupied with questions such as "Did I minister enough? Was my quiet time satisfactory? Did I do enough good and avoid sin enough? Was God pleased with my performance?"

On days when I did well by my own measure, I still felt empty and insecure. How could I be sure I'd done enough? How did I know He approved of me? Worst of all were the days when I sinned or failed or was weak or needy or hurting or doubting—those days were dreadful. Because I thought I was supposed to serve Jesus rather than let Him serve me, I tried to take care of my sins and hurts myself. I applied all the self-discipline, Bible knowledge, willpower, common sense, and perseverance I had, but it didn't work. Even if I got through that day's crisis, I did it in my own strength and felt distant from God. I was totally missing out on the deep closeness and security that comes from trusting in my Shepherd's unconditional, no-strings-attached love and care.

When I eventually realized I was doing God no favor by shutting Him out when I needed Him most—that He actually longed to be there for me no matter what condition I found myself in—the way I thought, felt, and prayed started to change. I let Him know when I felt harassed and helpless, when I needed compassion and comfort, when I was tempted to wander, even when I actually had wandered and was ready to be found. I'd never known someone who loved me that unconditionally, whom I could trust to be there for me no matter what kind of predicament I found myself in.

But that wasn't all. I was also blown away by how clearly God knew and cared about bad shepherding. Like many people, I'd had experiences with people in authority who were supposed to care for me and didn't. I hadn't realized how those experiences had caused me to form inaccurate perceptions of God. For example, based on some bad shepherding I'd received, I had come to believe certain lies about how life worked and I projected them onto my relationship with God—lies such as, "There's no one to defend me, so I have to defend myself" and "You need to perform and work hard if you want to be noticed and loved." As I opened my heart to talk to the Shepherd of my soul about my hurts and struggles, He reminded me about these bad shepherding experiences and helped me see how they had distorted my view of Him. He encouraged me to invite Him into these painful memories to show me how a good shepherd would care for me. And in this faithful, patient way, He restored—and continues to restore—both my soul and my view of Him.

RESPOND TO GOD

Which discovery of your Good Shepherd resonated most with you? That God wants to shepherd you, tenderly caring for you and meeting your needs? Or that God wants to be your *Good* Shepherd, healing the places where you have received neglectful or abusive shepherding? Based on your answer, select one of the following prayer prompts as the basis for a conversation with God your Shepherd. You can choose one for each day, or you may choose to use the same one for both days. You decide.

PRAYER RESPONSE 1: A Sheep Needs a Shepherd

a. Mark any of the following that you have felt at some time in the last two months.

harassed	afraid
taken advantage of	hurting
lost	stupid
needy	tired
helpless	wounded
stuck	broken
threatened	

b. Based on what you are discovering about the Good Shepherd, how do you think He feels about what you've experienced?

c. Choose something you marked and use it as the starting point for a conversation with your Shepherd. Tell Jesus what happened and how you've been feeling. Invite Him to reveal how He would like to shepherd you. Summarize what you talked about.

PRAYER RESPONSE 2: Receiving the Good Shepherd

If you've experienced bad shepherding, you can take it to the Good Shepherd and receive His shepherding. You don't have to continue to endure the hurt. There is a straightforward way to do this. (Note: If this prayer response doesn't seem to apply to you or if you're not ready to tackle it yet, feel free to skip it. You can always revisit it later.)

a. Tell Jesus about the wounding you (the "sheep") experienced, especially mentioning wounds that haven't yet healed. Wounds take different forms; they may include painful emotions you experience privately (feelings of abandonment, fear, sadness, anxiety, and so on) or troubling emotions that spill over onto others (anger, irritation, negativity, criticism) or both. Don't be afraid of these emotions if they surface as you talk with Him. He cares and wants to bring healing.

b. Ask Jesus how He wants to meet you. Remember, He speaks to His sheep; they know His voice. He may bring to mind a picture (maybe He will carry the hurting lamb close to His heart or pour soothing oil on the sheep's head; maybe He will chase a wolf away or kill it; maybe He will call the sheep by name and speak something personal and tender to it). Very likely He will speak a healing truth into the place of pain.

c. Respond to Jesus about whatever you sense Him doing or saying.

For example, if He reveals a lie you believed (such as, "You have to perform if you want to be loved"), agree with Him that you have believed that lie and ask Him what truth He has for you instead. Also ask Him to show you if you have sinned in any way as a result of the lie you believed, and then ask for and receive His forgiveness.

If He cares for you in some way (applying soothing oil, carrying the sheep, speaking tenderly to it), tell Him how His care for you makes you feel and ask for His help to fully receive the healing He is offering.

Respond to Him about whatever you sense Him doing as you bring your hurts to Him.

CONTINUE THE CONVERSATION

Each new facet of God you discover will open up new ways of talking with Him and enjoying Him. To help you explore these new ways of talking, I'll finish each study of a facet of God's character with a summary to help you interact with God and continue the conversation with Him (see "Our Good Shepherd," following). I've also left space for you to add notes about your personal discoveries.

Long after you've finished this study, these summaries can help you engage with God. In fact, I'd suggest you copy them and keep them accessible as a reminder of how you can relate with God in new ways.

For the remaining days before your group meeting, ask the Shepherd how He would like to interact with you. Then choose one of the suggestions in the summary as a way of starting your conversation with Him.

Jot notes here about your prayer times each day or journal these conversations. Either way, it will be encouraging to have a record of the way your relationship with God is growing and deepening.

KNOWING THE GOD YOU PRAY TO

Our Good Shepherd
My Good Shepherd . . .

Provides for me; gives rest and restoration; comforts and calms; leads and guides; protects, guards, and defends; keeps me company; heals; carries; rescues; seeks after and finds me when I'm lost; knows me personally; speaks to me by name; gives life; sacrifices for me.

Key Truths About Our Good Shepherd

- The sheep don't serve the Shepherd; He is the one who serves, provides, protects, and cares.
- Receiving God's *good* shepherding is the antidote to the damaging, bad shepherding we've experienced.
- Our self-sufficiency blocks Jesus from getting to shepherd us.

Add your own notes:

Praying Throughout the Day

- Talk to God as your Shepherd whenever you need to depend on Him to care for you.
- Ask Him for whatever you need that a shepherd would provide.
- Praise Him for His willingness to shepherd you.

Names to Use in Prayer

- My Shepherd, Good Shepherd
- Great Shepherd of the sheep (see Hebrews 13:20)
- Shepherd of my soul (see 1 Peter 2:25)
- God who has been my shepherd all my life (see Genesis 48:15)
- Yahweh-Rohi (God's name in Psalm 23:1; *Rohi* means "shepherd")

Scriptures to Pray

- Psalm 23; Luke 15:1-7; John 10:1-17,25-27

Pictures to Pray With

- Shepherd carrying lamb on shoulders or close to heart
- Shepherd defending sheep from wolves, bears, or lions
- Shepherd pouring soothing oil on wounded sheep's head
- Shepherd relaxing with sheep in a lush pasture by a babbling brook
- Shepherd heading out in a storm to find a lost sheep

Conversation Starters

- *Stress.* "I feel so anxious about _____. Will You lead me by Your peaceful, quiet waters?"
- *Fear.* "I'm scared. Will You protect me?"
- *Confusion / Decision Making.* "I'm confused about _____. I feel like a lost lamb. Will You guide me?"
- *Spiritual warfare, temptation, or mistreatment.* "I feel so vulnerable. Shepherd, please fight off the wolves snarling and snapping at me."
- *Comfort.* "I'm sad about _____. I need Your comfort, Shepherd of my soul."
- *Companionship.* "I'm lonely today, Jesus. Thanks that You want to be with me. How can we keep company together right now?"
- *Need to feel known, valued, and loved.* "My Shepherd, I'm so glad You understand my longings and take them seriously. Please meet

my needs for _____ right now."

- *Food, housing, finances, and other basic needs.* "Because You are my Shepherd, I don't have to worry about basic needs. Will You please supply the _____ I lack?"
- *Forgiveness.* "I've blown it, Jesus, and I'm sorry. Will You please get me unstuck and wash me clean again?"
- *Freedom from harassment, mistreatment, or oppression.* "Lord, You know all about the _____ I feel. How do You want to demonstrate Your compassion for me right now?"
- *Healing (physical, emotional, spiritual).* "Anoint me with Your healing oil, my Shepherd. I need Your touch in _____. Make me whole."
- *Help with tendencies to stray.* "I'm prone to wandering off, Yaweh-Rohi. I can't keep myself on the path, so will You show me how to keep in step with You today?"
- *Loved ones who are lost, wandering, or in danger.* "Thank You for loving and seeking out even one lamb that strays. Would you please bring _____ safely home?"
- *Rest.* "I'm so tired I can barely keep going. How do You want me to notice Your green pastures and quiet waters so I can rest?"
- *To be carried.* "I can't continue on my own. Shepherd, please carry me during this next stretch of the trail."

Add your own notes:

Summary from Lesson 2, *Knowing the God You Pray* by Cynthia Bezek. ©2015, Prayer-Shop Publishing.

Our Creator

FEEL FREE TO WORK through the lesson at your own pace. Just remember that the key to this study is prayer, so be sure to leave time for the prayer portions. Set appointments with yourself on your calendar if that would be helpful.

Have you noticed the rhythm we're using for the lessons? Each one starts by asking you to open yourself up to God and invite Him to do the study with you. Then, in the "Discover Who God Is" section, you go to Scripture and explore that aspect of God. Finally, the prayer responses bring the ideas home by showing you how to use them to talk with God. This sequence of "open, discover, and respond" is a basic one you can use whenever you read or study the Bible.

Suggestions for Pacing the Lesson

I'm giving you two possible ways to work through this week's material.

Days 1–3: Work through the "Discover Who God Is" questions.
Days 4–5: Do two of the "Respond to God" prayer exercises.
Days 6–7: Try one of the "Continue the Conversation" suggestions.

As an alternative, you could intersperse the prayer responses into your time of working through the questions. If you'd like to do that, try this plan:

Days 1–2: Work through questions 1–4 and prayer response 1 or 2.

Days 3–4: Work through questions 5–6 and prayer response 3.

Day 6: Work through question 7 and do prayer response 4.

Day 7: Try a remaining prayer response or one of the "Continue the Conversation" suggestions.

Over the years, I've gotten to know a number of artistic and creative people. One thing they all have in common is that they're proud of their creations. They call them their "babies"—and with good reason. They've labored to select just the right images, words, details, and designs. To their eyes, their works are masterpieces. If a callous reviewer, editor, or critic suggests their efforts could use improvement, some will react like mama bears. I don't think they could be more offended if someone suggested their actual flesh-and-blood kids were bald and bug-eyed and could use a tattoo to enhance their appearance.

As an author, I understand where they're coming from. I put hours of love and labor into the pieces I write. I don't want anything to corrupt or distort the messages I so carefully craft. When I've finished a work to my satisfaction, I want it to get out to the world and accomplish what I created it to do. Seeing a written work communicate grace, truth, and hope gives me incredible delight. My husband was an inventor, and I have friends who are artists and musicians. They, too, delight in and are protective of the works they create.

In a very small way, thinking about how people who create feel about their creations has helped me to understand a little bit more about God.

OPEN UP TO GOD

1. As you did last week, begin by inviting God to teach you about Himself. You may borrow this prayer or use your own words:

God, please help me to become quiet so I can focus on getting to know You better as my Creator. I have faith that You delight in being known, and I put aside my preconceived ideas of who I think You are so You can reveal Yourself as You truly are. Please open my heart and mind to knowing You personally as my Creator.

DISCOVER WHO GOD IS

Throughout Scripture, God uses a variety of names and titles to identify Himself as one who creates. He's an Architect and Builder (see Hebrews 11:10), Author (see Acts 3:15), Creator (see Isaiah 40:28), Gardener (see John 15:1), Maker (see Psalm 95:6), and Potter (see Isaiah 64:8). When I think of God as Creator, I enjoy using a few more names that, though they are not explicitly noted in Scripture, are biblical. God is also the *Source, Restorer, ReMaker,* and *ReCreator*. I'll be using many of these names and titles throughout this lesson. In every case, I am referring to the facet of God that has to do with Him being the creative source behind everything that exists.

It would be impossible to do any kind of comprehensive study of God in this role, so we'll focus on discovering who He is as our personal Designer and Creator. As you consider these Scripture passages, remember that our goal isn't traditional information gathering; we're out to discover God so we can relate to Him.

GOD'S DELIGHT IN HIS CREATION

2. Though you're probably familiar with the story, read again about God as the one who creates people.

Read the following passages slowly and meditatively. The first account is drawn from Genesis 1–2 in *The Message*. I hope seeing the story in this format makes some of the familiar words fresh for you.

Mark any places where the ideas and emotions listed in the margin sparkle and glimmer (don't get wrapped up in finding them all or figuring out the "right" place where the concept is seen; the list merely gives you an idea of the kinds of things to look for). Invite God to read with you: "Creator, I want to know more about You and what creating me was like. Help me to see Your actions and feel Your emotions with You." *(See chart on page 45.)*

3. Those passages crackle with the energy and delight that comes with creating something. It's obvious that God, the ultimate Creator, has feelings about what He has made! Let's explore more of how God feels toward us.

Read Psalm 121:1-8 and Isaiah 43:1-7 twice. The first time through, just read the passage to familiarize yourself with it. Then go back and read the passages again. As you do, ask God to highlight what He does that demonstrates how He cares for you, His handcrafted creation. Write down those actions, personalizing each one (I've done a sample for you). Invite God's interaction: "God, my Maker, help me see and feel in the core of my being the way You feel about me, Your handiwork."

Psalm 121:1-8

> v. 2 – My Maker helps me.
> v. 3 – My Creator will not let my foot slip.

Isaiah 43:1-7

As you read, watch for who God is; try to sense His feelings about His creation. Notice also how His creation responds to Him.

Mark places of . . .

Intention

Joy

Wonder

Attentiveness

Tenderness

Importance

Caring

Generosity

Excitement

Pleasure

Approval

Delight

Craftsmanship

God handcrafts a special creation:

This is the story of how it all started, of Heaven and Earth when they were created.

God spoke: "Let us make human beings in our image, make them reflecting our nature so they can be responsible for the fish in the sea, the birds in the air, the cattle, and, yes, Earth itself, and every animal that moves on the face of Earth."

God formed Man out of dirt from the ground and blew into his nostrils the breath of life. The Man came alive—a living soul!

God said, "It's not good for the Man to be alone; I'll make him a helper, a companion." God put the Man into a deep sleep. As he slept he removed one of his ribs and replaced it with flesh. God then used the rib that he had taken from the Man to make Woman and presented her to the Man.

The Man said, "Finally! Bone of my bone, flesh of my flesh! Name her Woman for she was made from Man."

God created human beings; he created them godlike, reflecting God's nature. He created them male and female.

God looked over everything he had made; it was so good, so very good!

—Genesis 1:26-27,31; 2:1,18,21-25 (MSG)

God handmakes every one of us:

Oh yes, you shaped me first inside, then out;
you formed me in my mother's womb.
I thank you, High God—you're breathtaking!
Body and soul, I am marvelously made!
I worship in adoration—what a creation!
You know me inside and out,
You know every bone in my body;
You know exactly how I was made, bit by bit, how I was
sculpted from nothing into something.
Like an open book, you watched me grow from conception
to birth; all the stages of my life were spread out before you, the
days of my life all prepared before I'd even lived one day.

—Psalm 139:13-16 (MSG)

4. Suppose you recently met someone who is okay with the idea of God creating but doesn't think it has much relevance today. "Sure, God created the entire earth," he tells you, "but then He stepped back and let natural processes take over." Based on the passages you just read and the notes you took, what would you tell him about his Creator as a Person who has personality, feelings, and commitment to what He has made? I've given you an example of how you might start.

I believe Our Creator cares so much about you and me that He used Himself as a pattern for us. He stamped you with His image, and it made Him happy to do it!

RELATING TO GOD AS OUR CREATOR

5. God is deeply connected to His creation. As you read Acts 17:24-28, try to put yourself into the story. Can you hear the apostle Paul pleading with the Greeks in Athens on their Creator's behalf? What does God want His creation—even those who have never heard of Him— to do? Why? (To answer "why," you may need to incorporate what you saw in the verses on the previous pages.)

6. As our loving Creator who planned every detail of our beings, God cares about how our lives turn out. We're so important to Him that

He wants us to let Him be involved in what happens to us. Meditate on the following pair of passages that contrast the ways we can choose to respond to our Creator God. Ponder them with God, and let the Holy Spirit speak creatively through them. Don't try to predict what He will do with you; allow Him to work personally, providing exactly what you need right now. He might point out an attitude He wants you to notice. He may speak to you about what life with Him is like. He may show you misconceptions you've held. He may tell you how He is pleased with you. He might call you to surrender in new ways.

Invite God to open your eyes: "Holy Spirit, will you read with me? Help me slow down and see You—and me—in these passages. Will you give me a new taste of what it's like to experience Your bringing Your words to life for me?"

Woe to those who go to great depths to hide their plans from the LORD, who do their work in darkness and think, "Who sees us? Who will know?"

You turn things upside down, as if the potter were thought to be like the clay! Shall what is formed say to him who formed it, "He did not make me"? Can the pot say of the potter, "He knows nothing"?

—Isaiah 29:15-17 (NIV)

For we are God's [own] handiwork (His workmanship), recreated in Christ Jesus, [born anew] that we may do those good works which God predestined (planned beforehand) for us [taking paths which He prepared ahead of time], that we should walk in them [living the good life which He prearranged and made ready for us to live].

—Ephesians 2:10 (AMP)

Make notes about what the Holy Spirit communicates to you:

GOD OUR REMAKER

Unlike anything a human creates, God's creations have minds of their own. Being clay in a Potter's hands sometimes creates tension for us. We wonder what kind of piece He's shaping us into and if we'll like it or not. Sometimes we resist the way He chooses to form us. We, God's creatures, can make unbelievable messes out of His masterpieces!

But we've been getting to know a Creator who is thoroughly invested in restoring His creation. I love the way the Amplified Bible translates Ephesians 2:10: "We are God's own handiwork, recreated in Christ Jesus."

A conversation with my artist friend Jack put this idea into perspective for me. When Jack takes his work to an exhibition, he's extremely careful in the way he wraps it, handles it, protects it, and transports it. Each painting is precious to him, and he doesn't want anything to happen to any of them. Even so, sometimes one of his pieces gets damaged. It may get smudged or the canvas may be torn. "What do you do with a marred painting?" I asked. Jack is an artist with thousands of creative ideas, so I supposed he might say he just threw away that painting and started a new one. But that's not the case.

"I repair it and find a way to remake it so that it will be even more beautiful and interesting than it was before," he replied, then mused a bit. What he said next surprised me: "Some of my most treasured works are ones I remade after they had been damaged in some way."

7. Read the following passages and notice what God is restoring and remaking in each. Write notes about whatever stands out to you about God's work as ReCreator, ReMaker, and Restorer. Pray, "ReMaker, I don't usually think of You as an artist restoring Your creation. Will you show me Yourself and Your joy as You bring life to damaged places?"

a. Psalm 51:10-12

b. Isaiah 61

c. 2 Corinthians 4:16-18

d. Colossians 3:1-10

e. Revelation 21:5

CYNTHIA'S DISCOVERIES ABOUT HER CREATOR

From as early as I can remember, I was taught about God as Creator. For years I've worshipped Him in this role, giving praise to the one who made all things beautiful, intricate, powerful, and majestic. I enjoyed nature with Him and thanked Him for sunsets and mountains and flowers and birds. But my conversations with Him as Creator weren't very personal until recently.

The shift took place when I started to notice the enormous pride God takes in His handiwork. Like any artist or creative person, He delights in what He has made and is making. I had never stopped to think about the fact that our Creator continues to gain pleasure from His creation. Furthermore, His reputation is staked on it. Isaiah 60:21 says that the work of His hands is intended to display His splendor. Is it any wonder He watches over it with such loving care?

Something stirred in me when I heard Jack talk about his paintings. "That's the kind of Artist I am, Child," I sensed God saying.

In that moment, I understood the concepts of restoration, renewal, and re-creation more personally than I'd known them before. When I am broken or damaged, whether through my own sin or another's sin against me, God looks on me with love. His beloved creation has been hurt. He is sad for the pain I've experienced, but He does not despair for a moment because nothing is beyond repair to Him—He's an absolute genius in making all things new!

I considered some of the damage in my life: things the enemy had stolen from me, breakages from living in a fallen world, and places that had been harmed through my sin, ignorance, and failure. I'd sometimes felt that damage could never be fixed. But realizing that God not only creates but also re-creates . . . well, that gave me huge hope and considerable joy! He didn't create me as a work of art only to abandon me when my life started getting messy. He could remake me no matter how ruined I felt. He's a master Potter who, if His workmanship becomes flawed in some way, can put it back on the wheel and reshape it into something beautiful.

Obviously these realizations about God are transforming how I pray. Instead of feeling as though I need to suck it up, accept my damages, and move on, I am now like a child taking a broken treasure to Daddy. In prayer, I gather up the broken pieces, lift them to my Creator, and ask Him what He wants to do with them. "How will You re-create this, God? Will You please restore and make something new and beautiful out of this mess?"

And He does. Let me give you an example. What follows is dialogue I had with God on my wedding anniversary a year and a half after my husband died. The non-italicized words are my exact words to God. The italicized words are what I believe I heard Him saying to me.

"Today is my twenty-fifth wedding anniversary, Father, and I'm alone. David didn't make it to this day. When we were young, I never dreamed of this. I thought I'd get my ring reset and we'd take a trip and we'd look forward to the fruits of older age together. But there's a whole new script instead. I still feel the loss, even though I thought I'd healed.

"What about my marriage? This anniversary? What do they mean? What do they accomplish?"

"This isn't a 'so that' kind of situation, child. It's not chemistry. It's art."

"Tell me more, Father."

"In chemistry, you carefully measure and precisely mix chemicals 'so that' you get a certain specific reaction. In art, you look at the materials available to you and then arrange them in ways—often unpredictable, out-of-the-box ways—that create beauty. In art, there are endless ways of putting together the materials. In chemistry, there's just one way—unless you want an explosion.

"Child, your life is a canvas, not a test tube. And I am the Artist, an incredible Artist. I can take the most unlikely materials and make unspeakable beauty from them. Your marriage—your life with David, both the good and the painful—is taking a beautiful place on your life canvas. If you look at it from a distance, you'll hardly even recognize it. But come up closer and you'll be amazed. Your marriage and all the hard stuff in it is still the same marriage, yet it is transformed into something lovely and meaningful. Share this with your artist friends and ask them to help you understand."

"I see some of what You're saying: All things work together for the good of those who love You and are called according to Your purposes."

"Yes, that's it. But don't get lost in spiritual talk, little one. This is real, very real. Your marriage—the joys, the disappointments, the sorrows—is being entirely redeemed. All of it. Not one part wasted. Not even the parts you regret and wish you could do over. I don't 'erase.' I refashion. And what I create— and re-create—is good. Your life is good, Cynthia. The tears aren't 'bad' and the laughter 'good.' It's all good.

"Oh, little one, I hear you. You're thinking that I sound like that Buddhist lady you talked to years back—'It's all good, even evil is good.' NO! That's not what I'm saying. I'm saying that I am greater than sin, sorrow, sickness, and death. The effects of the Fall are the wages of sin. I'm not saying they are essentially good. What I am saying is that when they are given to Me—as you have given them to Me—I transform them into beauty and goodness.

"Child, herein lies the peace: in being able to hand Me any material, anything at all, even what looks ugly or worthless to you, and asking Me to incorporate it into something beautiful in the canvas of your life."

Can you imagine how God's perspective changed the way I viewed my grief and disappointment? Knowing that He was going to bring beauty out of it all gave me new hope—joy even. He wants to do that for you, too, with whatever broken pieces you have to offer Him.

RESPOND TO GOD

As we mentioned in the previous lesson, we never want to learn information about God and then walk away as if the goal has been satisfied. Instead, we want to let what we've discovered soak in and affect how we relate with and talk to our Creator.

If you haven't already begun using the following prayer responses as you have worked through the questions above, read through them now and choose two responses to help you talk with your Creator God.

PRAYER RESPONSE 1: "I am Your creation, in whom You delight."

a. Reflect on how God says He cares for you, His creation. If you absolutely trusted Him to care for you in these ways, how would it affect the way you talked to your Maker? (Check all that apply.)

_____ I'd talk to Him more about my everyday needs and concerns.

_____ I'd worry less and probably say, "Thank You, God," more.

_____ I'd be more secure in His love, so my prayers would be bolder and more confident.

_____ I'd love Him even more and tell Him so.

_____ I'd enjoy talking to Him about the ways I saw Him caring for me each day.

_____ I'd talk to Him more about others who need His care because He loves them, too.

_____ I'd be more aware of His presence with me, so I'd probably include Him more in whatever was going on in my life.

_____ Other:

b. Turn the response(s) you checked into a prayer. Tell God what you feel. If there is an area in which you'd like to know and enjoy Him better, tell Him that, too. Then listen for His response and respond back to Him. Summarize your conversation here:

PRAYER RESPONSE 2: "I am fearfully and wonderfully made."

Talk to God about the incredible way He designed you inside and out—mentally, physically, emotionally, and spiritually. Consider adapting the words from Psalm 139 quoted at the beginning of this lesson. Thank Him for making you.

It's possible, however, that you are not able to fully appreciate some aspect of how He made you. Many of us struggle with that. If that's where you are, here's a way to talk to Him about it. I strongly suggest you write down your conversation with God to get the most out of this exercise.

a. Tell Him what aspect of who you are or how you are made is hard for you to accept or enjoy. Be completely honest.

b. Ask God to help you understand why you tend to reject this aspect of yourself. There are often concrete reasons we form negative opinions of ourselves. Sometimes our opinions come from demeaning comments someone made when we were young. Sometimes they come from our culture saying we must possess certain features in order to be attractive. Sometimes they come from comparing ourselves with others and coming up short, in our estimation. There could be other root causes as well.

As you ask God to help you understand where your self-rejection came from, *expect* Him to show you. Sit quietly with Him and allow Him time to bring to mind a memory, thought, feeling, picture, Scripture, or whatever else He chooses to give you insight. Record what you sense Him sharing with you.

c. Interact with God about what He shows you. If you have questions or need clarification or confirmation about what He says, ask Him. Record both your questions and His responses.

d. Respond to what He shows you. For example, if you've let someone else's untrue and demeaning words define you, tell Him you are sorry you believed those lies. If you bought into a lie fed to you by advertisements or media, ask His forgiveness for believing that lie. If you compared yourself negatively to someone else (appreciating how God made the other person but criticizing how He made you), confess that comparison as wrong. Write down your responses to God.

e. Now ask God to show you what is true and to help you embrace that. Write down what He says and your response.

f. Ask Him to re-create your mind and heart so You can see, accept, and enjoy yourself the way He, your Maker, does.

g. Finish your time by thanking Him for what He has shown you and for how He lovingly designed you.

PRAYER RESPONSE 3: "I am the clay, You are the Potter."

Theologically, most of us can probably agree that because God made us, He has the right to decide what happens with us. But when the rubber of His Sovereign ownership meets the road of our desires and choices, it can sometimes be hard to yield to the ways He wants to shape and form us.

a. How does the Creator's ownership of you make you feel? Check as many of the following statements as describe your feelings:

- ☐ I'm glad He cares that much to be so closely involved with me.
- ☐ I'm nervous about it; frankly, I don't want to be micromanaged.
- ☐ If I could really trust Him to do a good job with me, I think I'd be a whole lot more relaxed and peaceful.
- ☐ If He can make something beautiful or useful out of the mess I've made with my life, He can go for it.
- ☐ I'm used to being independent; I'm not sure I'm ready for Him to be that involved with me.
- ☐ I'm okay with Him directing my life, if only I could be sure I was actually in step with His plans for me.
- ☐ Other:

b. Did you check anything you are uncomfortable admitting to? Don't worry—you're just being honest with a God who desires truth in our inner parts (see Psalm 51:6). Being honest with yourself and God is the first step toward life-giving change. Instead of trying harder or pretending you feel differently than you do, have a conversation with Him about how you feel. Here are some talking points to help you:

- Describe to the Potter what part of your life you have difficulty releasing to His hands. (Keep in mind that He, more than anyone, understands and is compassionate about your weaknesses [see Psalm 103:13-14], so don't be afraid to tell Him about your struggle.)
- Tell Him why you think you are fearful or reluctant to let Him take charge of this part of you. If you aren't sure why, ask Him to show you, then listen for (and write down) what you sense Him saying.

c. Now ask Him to show you (or remind you) about who He truly is in regard to your situation. Is there something about Him that could help you release control so He can work in you?

What do you think He might be saying to you? Listen for His reassurance. Expect Him to speak to you as a loving Father would speak to His well-loved child who is struggling. Write down what you hear.

d. Respond to what God is saying to you.

PRAYER RESPONSE 4: "Creator-Daddy, will you fix it?"

Is there something in you that is marred, stained, or broken—by your own sin, another's sin against you, or the general wear and tear of life? a. What is it?

b. Ecclesiastes 3 says that God oversees everything under heaven—including things uprooted, torn, and dying—and makes everything "beautiful in its time" (verse 10).

Reread the Scriptures in question 7 on page 48 about God's work as Restorer and ReCreator. Ask the Holy Spirit to open your heart as you read slowly and meditatively, letting the words soak into your heart as well as your mind. Ask God to help you *feel* His love, care, and longing for you as Your Maker and ReMaker.

Ask Him to highlight personally one verse or passage for you. Which one did He give you?

c. Read this passage two or three more times, allowing for several minutes of silence between each reading. During the silence, turn the words over in your heart and mind and invite the Holy Spirit to apply them to your needs. Try not to go into Bible study mode, focusing on what you need to do to apply the Scripture; instead, think of the verses as God's loving invitation to you. Ask Him what He wants to do for you—how *He* wants to work in your life. Accept His invitation to re-create you and heal whatever is broken or wounded. Note what He says to you in the readings.

Reading One:

Reading Two:

Reading Three:

d. Finish your time by thanking God for His passion to restore and renew His creation. Share your feelings with Him openly. Listen to His response. Talk to Him about whatever He says.

CONTINUE THE CONVERSATION

Revisit any of the prayer responses from this lesson that you didn't have time for or need to spend more time with. You can also choose prompts from the following summary to help you enjoy conversations with God as your Creator.

You may have noticed that many of the prayer responses this week addressed inaccurate or incomplete perceptions of God as our Creator. You may want to spend more time praying in those areas, paying particular attention to the ones that counteract your default misunderstandings about God. For example, in lesson 1, I mentioned my default perception of God as Judge and Ruler, so, of course, I had no problem acknowledging that God was my Potter. However, I particularly needed to complete the picture of God as Creator by understanding His hands-on care and restoration.

Obviously, there are more prayer suggestions than you can use now, so don't expect to cover them all right away. Instead, ask your Creator how He would like to interact with you, and then choose one of the suggestions as a way of starting your conversation with Him.

Jot notes about your prayer times or journal the conversations. Either way, it will be encouraging to have a record of how your relationship with God is growing and deepening.

Misperceptions of God as Creator

Here are some misperceptions we are particularly prone to about this facet of God:

- Thinking that God created the world but will not intervene in it (this is deistic thinking, which Christians can fall into)
- Praising Him for what we see around us in nature while discounting His incredible work in designing us
- Cringing at the picture of God as a Potter because we view God as an uncaring authority
- Failing to recognize His good and loving ownership of us as the Potter
- Perceiving God as a Christianized Mother Earth or Mother Nature whose primary interest is how we care for the planet
- Failing to grasp or allow the Creator's ongoing re-creation, renewing, and restoring

If you are particularly prone to one of these misconceptions, you might want to spend more time in that area of prayer.

KNOWING THE GOD YOU PRAY TO

Our Creator

My Creator . . .

Fashioned me in love, created a beautiful world for me to live in and enjoy, and remakes what gets broken, stained, or lost in the course of living in a fallen world. He watches over me with constant, loving attentiveness. What He has made brings Him glory and delight.

Key Truths About Our Creator

- What God makes is good. He designed me exactly the way He wants me to be, and it is good.
- Because God made me, I belong to Him and He gets to decide what is best for me.
- Although brokenness mars us, God is ReMaker as well as Maker; He can restore anything into the beautiful masterpiece He intended.

Add your own notes:

Praying Throughout the Day

- Worship God for the beauty of His creation: a singing bird, a gorgeous sunset, a laughing child.
- Remind yourself that you are not your own; He made you. Then ask your Creator what *He* wants for you in various circumstances.
- When you find yourself looking for affirmation or approval from people, turn to God your Maker and ask Him to tell you how He

loves you and delights in you; ask Him to help you believe and receive His love and affection.
- When you feel stained or broken, tell Him about it and ask Him to restore or re-create you.

Names to Use in Prayer

- Maker, ReMaker (see Psalm 95:6; Revelation 21:5)
- Creator, ReCreator (see Isaiah 40:28; 2 Corinthians 5:17)
- Potter (see Isaiah 64:8)
- Author of Life (see Acts 3:15)
- Builder; ReBuilder (see Hebrews 11:10)
- Gardener (see John 15:1)
- Restorer (see Psalm 23:3; 51:12)

Scriptures to Pray

- Psalm 95:1-7; 100; 121

Pictures to Pray With

- Artist painting on a beautiful canvas
- Potter lovingly and attentively working with soft clay on a wheel
- Father with open hands receiving the broken pieces His child lifts to Him to fix
- Gardener digging, transplanting, weeding, pruning in a peaceful garden
- Architect drawing up masterful designs and plans
- Restoration expert rebuilding a masterpiece

Conversation Starters

- *Worship.* "Creator of heaven and earth, Your creation is . . ."
- *Need.* "Nothing is too hard for You, Designer of the universe. Please work creatively in . . ."

- *Damage and brokenness.* "God my Maker and ReMaker, I feel broken. How would You like to rework this brokenness into something beautiful?"
- *Worry.* "Author of life, I am anxious about _____. But it helps me to know how attentive You are to me simply because You made me. You delight in me! Please help me rest in Your care."
- *Surrender.* "Restorer God, I've made a mess of things. I've forgotten that You made me and I am not my own. Would You please forgive my independence, put me back on track, show me Your plans for my life, and restore the damage I've caused?"
- *Correction and Cleaning.* "Gardener, the garden of my life is overgrown and weedy. I trust You. Will You please come in and bring order and beauty?"
- *Self-Worth.* "God who fashioned me in my mother's womb, I want to delight in the way You made me, but honestly I don't like _____ about me very much. Will You please help me see myself the way You designed me to be and help me to accept myself?"
- *Decision-Making.* "Architect and Designer, I know You have planned my life exquisitely. Will You show me Your blueprints for me regarding _____ so I follow Your design and not my own?"

Add your own notes:

Summary from Lesson 3, *Knowing the God You Pray To*, by Cynthia Bezek. ©2015, PrayerShop Publishing.

Our Mighty-to-Save God

HAVE YOU BEEN getting to the "Continue the Conversation" portion at the end of each of these lessons? There I'm intentionally giving you much less direction for how to pray. That's because the prayer starters on the summary pages are great ways for you to personalize the principles you are learning. I'd like to encourage you to work them into your daily life so that you will carry them with you long after you have finished this study.

Pace yourself this week to allow yourself time to spend at least a day or two using the prayer starters.

Suggestions for Pacing the Lesson

Days 1–3: Work through the questions.
Days 4–5: Do two of the "Respond to God" prayer exercises.
Days 6–7: Pray from the "Continue the Conversation" summary
pages for one or two days. If you have time, also do the
third "Respond to God" exercise.

As a cradle evangelical, I knew from as long as I could remember that the most important decision people would ever make was to accept Jesus as their personal Savior. Until recently, I still had one primary understanding of being "saved." It meant that because Jesus died for my sins and I put my faith in Him, I would be saved from God's wrath and one day go to heaven. When I thought about Jesus as my

Savior, I thought of His death on the cross, which secured my eternal destiny. But when I started to understand the fuller meanings of "Savior," these wonderful discoveries enormously changed the ways I relate to God and talk with Him.

This week we're going to focus on our God, who is mighty to save. Please know I consider salvation, in the sense we primarily speak of it, central to our lives with God. I do not want to diminish it in any way; I will always be infinitely grateful that Jesus made eternal life with Him possible. However, because salvation from sin and its penalty is something we talk of and explain regularly, I'm not going to cover it in this lesson. Instead, we will look at a broader picture of God's desire to save and rescue us.

OPEN UP TO GOD

1. Invite God, your Savior, to teach you about Himself. You may borrow this prayer if you like or use your own words:

God, I'm thankful You made a way in Jesus to save me from my sins and rescue me from being separated from You. I need saving in other ways, too—"everyday" salvations. Please open my heart and mind to embrace the many ways You want to save me. I want to relate to You more fully and enjoy You for who You are.

DISCOVER WHO GOD IS

2. Scripture provides us with a long list of God's saving ways and names. An example of His salvation shows up on nearly every page of the Bible (don't take my word for it—check it out!). The following passages show just a handful of God's ways of saving. For as many of the references as you have time for, look up the passage and describe the

salvation you find mentioned.

a. Psalm 34:4

Deliverer from fears

b. Psalm 34:17

Delivers from troubles

c. Psalm 86:13

Delivered from the grave

d. Matthew 1:21

Save from sins

e. Romans 5:9

Saved from God's wrath

f. Galatians 1:3-4

rescue us from evil

g. Colossians 1:13

rescued us from dominion of darkness

h. 2 Thessalonians 3:2-3

Protect from evil one.

i. 2 Timothy 3:10-11

rescued from persecutions

j. 2 Timothy 4:16-18

Will rescue from every evil attack

k. James 5:15 (Note: Though your Bible might translate it differently, in this verse, the Greek word for what the Lord will do is *sozo*, "save" [see "Some Background on Salvation"].)

deliver from sin.

l. 2 Peter 2:9

rescue from trials.

Some Background on Salvation

The Bible talks of salvation, "the act of saving," in very broad terms. The word is used for all kinds of saving: physical, spiritual, emotional, relational.

The Old Testament Hebrew word for "save" is *yasha*. It includes the ideas of delivering, protecting, preserving, rescuing, defending against reproach and condemnation, granting success, helping, and fighting on behalf of.

The New Testament Greek word for "save" is *sozo*. It brings in the idea of saving from sin and its penalty but also encompasses the ideas of healing, delivering from temptation and the evil one, making whole, restoring, and rescuing from physical, emotional, and spiritual dangers.

Many other words besides *yasha* and *sozo* are used to describe God's nature and desire to deliver, rescue, help, protect, and defend. In fact, the name *Jesus* means "salvation." It is the Greek form of the Hebrew *Joshua* (*Yeshua*), which has been translated in a variety of ways, including "God saves," "God is salvation," "God is a saving-cry," "God is a cry for help," or "God is my help." It is clear that salvation is not just something God *does*, it is who He *is*.

3. Isn't it amazing to see all the things God saves us from? Until we see a list like the one we just created, we can be unaware of the scope of salvation God wants to provide. God's desire to save us is good news! In the following space, "preach" the good news to yourself. The psalmists sometimes did this; they would remind themselves of the goodness of God. Fill in the blank with your name and then, looking back over your list above, continue the description by talking to yourself about who God is for you.

" _____Crystal_____, you have a God who saves, whose very name speaks of rescue! Your God wants to deliver you from all your fears. He would like to . . . be my peace giver, my comforter, my strength.

WHEN GOD DOESN'T SEEM TO BE SAVING

Despite all these encouraging and hopeful ways God saves us, I have to admit that sometimes it hasn't seemed as though God was protecting, helping, saving, or defending me. In those times, I often reacted by talking with Him less—or at least by avoiding those painful topics when I did talk with Him. As a result, our relationship suffered.

My journey out of despairing of God's salvation into genuine, "rubber-meets-the-road" hope in Him is more than I can tell here. But here's a piece of it: I had to come to terms with the fact that God never promised to prevent me from experiencing pain. His protection is about helping me endure through it with my love for Him intact. This understanding doesn't make hardships hurt any less, but it does mean I'm less likely to feel abandoned or mistreated or betrayed when they come. I realize that painful times and God's love can—and often do—coexist.

Here's another piece: God works on a different timetable than I would often like. That doesn't make God less faithful or His promises less true. It may just mean that He's working from an eternal, rather than temporal perspective.

I also learned that even though God may seem unresponsive about an area where I think I need saving, He is not unresponsive to me in general. I don't have to avoid Him because He doesn't seem to be coming through for me. If I go to Him and pour out my heart, telling Him how afraid or needy or hurt I am, I can almost always sense His responding to me and pulling me close to Himself.

4. One of the chief ways the enemy can get in the middle of your relationship with God is by causing you to lose confidence in God's love and goodness. To prevent him from doing this, it's a great idea to keep reminding yourself of God's power and desire to save you.

That way, when you feel discouraged and your hope of being rescued starts to wane, you don't have to depend on how your circumstances look or feel. You can remind yourself of who God really is and what He really is like. The following Scripture passages are just three of many that emphasize God's longing to save you and His firm and clear commitment to you.

> We praise you, Lord God! You treat us with kindness day after day, and you rescue us. (Psalm 68:19, CEV)

> The Lord [earnestly] waits [expecting, looking, and longing] to be gracious to you; and therefore He lifts Himself up, that He may have mercy on you and show lovingkindness to you. (Isaiah 30:18, AMP)

> The faithful love of the Lord never ends! His mercies never

cease. Great is his faithfulness; his mercies begin afresh each morning. I say to myself, "The Lord is my inheritance; therefore, I will hope in him!" The Lord is good to those who depend on him, to those who search for him. So it is good to wait quietly for salvation from the Lord." (Lamentations 3:22-26, NLT)

a. According to what you just read, how often can you reasonably expect God to save you?

every day.

b. Underline words or phrases in the verses that assure you that God is not impatient with your needs or begrudging about saving you.

c. How can receiving God's loving words and attention be a "rescue," even if He doesn't immediately relieve your circumstances? *You can hold on to His promises and belive that He will do what He says He will do.*

A Note about the Study: You may remember that a core goal of this study is to equip you to be able to discover more facets of God on your own. I want to point out again the simple process we've been using:

(1) open ourselves up to God,

(2) discover God in His Word, and

(3) relate with Him about what we've seen.

As you divide up the lesson over a week, be aware of moving through these steps each day. Be sure to start by opening yourself up to God, then discover Him, and finally make sure you don't leave the time without responding to Him. If you like, you could do Prayer Response 1 now.

MAKING ROOM FOR GOD TO SAVE

5. Sometimes I don't experience God's saving because I haven't put myself in a place to let Him come through for me. Yes, there are times He intervenes and rescues me even before I ask Him, but His help does not always come automatically. He likes to be looked to and asked, which means I need to be willing to acknowledge my need, believe that He truly wants to help me, and invite Him into my situation. Sometimes it even means I need to be willing to wait for and trust His timing.

Two Old Testament kings provide helpful examples here. Unlike so many kings of ancient Israel and Judah, both men in this father-son pair were considered "good guys." They followed God and were commended by Him (see 2 Chronicles 14:2-6; 17:3-6). Yet they showed two different approaches to asking God for salvation.

Read about Asa, the father, and then Jehoshaphat, his son, and make notes about:

- Opportunities they had to ask God to save them
- How they did or didn't use these opportunities
- How God responded to each one and what He felt about what they'd done

Remember that our goal in this study is to enter into relationship with God through His Word, not just search for information. To do this, I find it helpful to bring all I know of myself to all I know of Him as I read. What I mean by this is that I try to place myself in the story and identify, as honestly as I can, what my thoughts, feelings, and actions would have been if the events were happening to me. I also try to pick up on what God is thinking, feeling, and doing. In between reading, I usually pray, "God, help me to know You better and relate to You more completely. Teach me how to connect with You." In this way, Scripture is not just about people in another culture who lived a very long time ago; it's also about God and me, right now.

Try to do this as you read. You might want to read the passages through once for an overview and then read again, more meditatively.

a. Asa (see 2 Chronicles 16)

b. Jehoshaphat (see 2 Chronicles 20:1-29)

RESPOND TO GOD

Choose two of the following prayer responses as the basis for a conversation with God your Savior.

PRAYER RESPONSE 1: Praying God's Word Back to Him

a. Pick one of the passages in question 4 one page ~~69~~ 72 and turn it into the start of a prayer to God your Savior. ("God, I see now that You are earnestly waiting, expecting, looking, and longing to be gracious to me . . .")

God, I See ~~the~~ now that you are good to those who depend on you, to those who search for you.

b. Then add to it by relating how you feel and think. You could tell Him how you feel about asking Him to rescue you, or you could tell Him about a specific area in which you need His salvation, or both!

It's hard sometimes to truly depend on you fully + truly search for you like I should.

c. After you've shared your thoughts and feelings, wait quietly. How do you sense God responding? Remember to listen for relationship, not just "answers." Write your conversation with God on separate paper or in your journal.

PRAYER RESPONSE 2: Addressing Hesitation

In the stories of Asa and Jehoshaphat, we saw that many times we don't turn to God when we need rescue.

a. Write down an area of your life in which you need rescue but hesitate to ask God for it. Here's a whole list of possibilities:

anger	guilt
anxiety	injustice
bad habits	loneliness
bitterness	lust
bondage	painful memories
condemnation	persecution
cynicism	physical danger
death	poor self-image
depression	practical needs
discouragement	rejection
doubt	resentment
emotional wounding	sickness
false accusation	sins
fears	spiritual attack
financial trouble	temptation
greed	troubled relationships

b. Tell God why it's hard to ask Him to save you in this area of need. If you don't know why it's hard, ask Him to tell you, and then listen quietly for His response. What will likely happen is that a lie or partial truth will come to mind. This is the Holy Spirit giving you insight. For example, you may have mistakenly believed something such as, "God helps those who help themselves" or "I was the one who messed up, so I don't deserve to be helped" or "Even if I ask, no one is going to help me so why bother?" If you are unsure that what you are sensing is really from God, ask Him, "God, I'm sensing _____. Is this really what You want me to pay attention to?" When you are learning to hear from God, He is more than willing to provide the help, clarification, and confirmation you need to be sure you're hearing from Him. (If you get stuck, you might need to come back to this on another day. This kind of listening can be difficult.)

c. Tell God what usually happens when you don't ask Him to save you (for example, attempting to save yourself somehow; going to others to save you; just ignoring, stuffing, or resigning yourself to your unmet need).

When you do these things instead of asking God to save you, how is your soul affected?

d. Ask God to show you why He wants to save you instead of having you try to handle it in one of the ways you just read. If you have trouble hearing from Him on this, try speculating about what you think He would say based on what you know about who He is and the kind of relationship He wants to have with you.

e. Discuss with Him how having Him save you would affect your relationship with Him. If the relational benefits of involving Him seem positive, tell Him so and thank Him for wanting that kind of relationship with you.

f. Are you ready to ask Him to save you yet? If so, go ahead and ask Him. Tell Him all about your need and how you feel about it. Ask Him to rescue you. Then listen for what He has to say to you. Listen for His heart as well as for any guidance He may give you, keeping in mind that He is as much about deepening His relationship with you as He is about meeting your immediate need.

PRAYER RESPONSE 3: A Song of Salvation

Throughout biblical history, when God delivered His people, they often responded with a joyful song or prayer of salvation. These songs or prayers were recorded and saved so future generations could recite or sing them and remind themselves of God's faithfulness and mighty acts of salvation.

For examples of these songs and prayers, look at the song sung by Moses, Miriam, and the Israelites in Exodus 15:1-21; Hannah's prayer in 1 Samuel 2:1-11; David's song in 2 Samuel 22; Mary's song in Luke 1:46-55; or the song of Moses in Revelation 15:3-4.

How has God saved you? Write your own prayer or song to praise Him for His faithfulness and celebrate your deliverance. Consider using one of the Scripture prayers or songs as a model. When you have crafted your prayer and have prayed or sung it to God, ask Him whom He would like you to share it with so another person (or those people) can rejoice with you and celebrate a God who saves. Then follow through and share it.

PRAYER RESPONSE 4: Knowing My True Savior

A study of God's salvation can cause us to raise all kinds of objections, often because we have misconceptions of what His salvation means. Following are several I have believed, along with some others that are common:

- Thinking that God's acting as Rescuer and Protector means He will never allow me to experience hardship and pain
- Believing that God wouldn't allow me to suffer if He really loved me
- Interpreting God's apparent lack of response as "the silent treatment" (that because He doesn't seem to be saving me in the area I'm asking Him to, He doesn't want to communicate with me at all)
- Expecting God to save me on my terms and in my timing
- Believing that "salvation" is for only certain kinds of trials (for example, only "spiritual" needs or only "big" things that responsible people cannot do for themselves)
- Believing that God's salvation must be deserved and that if I've been irresponsible or disobedient, I shouldn't anticipate Him intervening
- Thinking that if God doesn't save me at my first call for help, I should probably give up and move on to Plan B
- Thinking I'll wear God out or irritate Him if I expect Him to rescue me too many times

a. Which ones have you believed?

b. How have these inaccurate or incomplete views of God affected your prayers? Your relationship with Him? If you don't know, ask the Holy Spirit to show you, and then wait for His response. He will probably bring to mind a specific memory or a familiar pattern of thought or behavior.

c. Ask God to forgive you for buying into damaging misperceptions of Him. Ask Him to tell you what is really true about Himself. Why is it important to Him that you know Him as He really is instead of how the enemy has slandered Him to you? Listen to His heart. Write down what you sense Him saying. If you have trouble hearing, feel free to speculate about what you think He might say based on what you know about Him and His desire for relationship with you.

d. Finish your conversation by responding to what He has said. This might mean thanking or praising Him, asking Him for help, or inviting Him into new areas of your life.

WHAT CYNTHIA DISCOVERED AND HOW THAT AFFECTED HER PRAYERS

As I pondered the breadth of God's salvation, I started seeing possibilities for letting Him into my life that I'd never seen before. If God really wanted to rescue and save me, well, I had plenty of ways to ask Him to do that! So my prayers started to broaden into new categories where ordinarily I would not have asked God to save.

Practical. Recently widowed, I missed the ways my once-healthy husband used to bail me out, such as helping me find my misplaced keys, taking care of the car so I wouldn't get stranded, fixing my computer when it crashed, and dealing with the IRS. It was easy to call to him for help. It was not as easy to ask God for those kinds of rescues, but I decided to try. Take the time the huge cottonwood tree in my backyard came down in an ice storm. It not only took out my fence but two adjacent fences as well. My tree was sprawled across my neighbors' yards, and their dogs could get out. I had to deal with this—quickly! I felt panicky and overwhelmed. It was on my shoulders to get this taken care of, but I didn't know where to start.

Then I remembered that God had promised to rescue me from all kinds of trials, so I talked to Him about it. "You are my Savior, right? Does that include trees? I can't even get out my back door—the tree is taking up my entire yard. I need to take care of it and soon! But how? I can't do this! How do You want to rescue me, Jesus?"

And He really did want to come to my aid. He showed me a truly creative way to find someone reliable to take care of the tree, something I never would have thought of. But more than that, He even worked out an opportunity to heal a strained relationship with a neighbor in the process. I'd never seen that part coming and was in complete awe of God's wisdom and power and delight in saving me from the tree and a poor relationship!

Spiritual. I used to try to deal with bad habits and sin patterns by reading Christian books and employing lots of self-discipline. After years of battling with some of the same habits and sins, however, I made little progress and just felt all the more hopeless and guilty.

I used to think salvation was only about being saved from the penalty of sin, but I realized now that it was for the temptation and bondage of sin, too. So I contacted a friend (being mindful of James 5:16, where we're told to confess sins to one another) and together we asked God to rescue me. Although God's full deliverance didn't come immediately, He did immediately start speaking to me about my struggles. He was full of love and understanding and brought healing to some root causes for those habits and sins—healing that sometimes I didn't even know I needed. As I continue to ask Him to save me, He is delivering me from patterns I've battled for decades! I don't have to do it alone because His name is Savior!

Emotional. After my husband died and my son was off at college, I found myself living alone for the first time ever. I didn't know what to do with all the quiet. In the evenings after work and especially on the weekends, I felt restless, incomplete, and adrift. In the past I would have told myself, *Deal with it*. I'd have found ways to fill up my time with activities. But now I remembered that part of God's saving work was to make me whole. I asked Him to fill the empty places.

He hasn't saved me overnight from loneliness. I still talk with Him about it often. But as I continue to ask Him for help instead of following my inclination to fill my life with busyness, I'm getting to know Him at a far deeper level. It feels really hopeful and good to have Him rescue my heart like this.

CONTINUE THE CONVERSATION

Keep talking with the God who delights to save us. If you'd like to do more of the prayer responses, go ahead and do the third or fourth one. Otherwise, choose some prayer starters from the following summary pages to help you enjoy conversations with God your Savior.

There are more prayer suggestions than you can use now, so don't expect to cover them all. Instead, each day ask your Savior how He would like to interact with you, and then choose one of the suggestions as a way of starting your conversation.

Jot notes about your prayer times on separate paper or journal these conversations so you can have a record of the way your relationship with God is growing and deepening.

KNOWING THE GOD YOU PRAY TO

Our Mighty-to-Save God
My Savior . . .

Longs for me to ask Him for help. He delivers, protects, preserves, rescues, defends against reproach and condemnation, grants success, and fights for me. He anticipates my coming to Him for rescue because He genuinely wants to have mercy on me. There is no need I'll ever have that won't qualify for His salvation. If I ask Him to save me (instead of trying to save myself), my relationship with Him will grow deeper and more secure. My Savior's very name, Jesus, means "salvation."

Key Truths About Our Savior

- God's salvation includes every aspect of my life—spiritual, physical, emotional, relational—everything!
- When I'm in trouble, the enemy works overtime to get me to doubt God's salvation. It's critical for me to remember the truth about my Savior because things are often not the way they appear.
- Acknowledging my need, asking for help, trusting in God's character, and actually expecting Him to save are ways I can actively make room for God's salvation.

Add your own notes:

Praying Throughout the Day

- For strength when you feel weak

- For peace and wholeness
- For deliverance from temptation, evil, and the evil one
- For protection from enemies
- For help in trials and difficulties
- For defense from harassment, mistreatment, or oppression
- For salvation from sin and its consequences

Names to Use in Prayer

- My Strength (see Psalm 18:1)
- My Deliverer (see Psalm 18:2)
- My Helper (see Psalm 27:9)
- My Defender (see Proverbs 23:11)
- My Refuge (see Deuteronomy 33:27)
- My Protector (see Psalm116:6)
- My Savior (see Psalm 18:46)
- Preserver of My Life (see Psalm 31:23)

Scriptures to Pray

- Psalms 25; 70; 91; Matthew 1:21; 6:13, Galatians 1:4; 1 Thessalonians 5:23-24

Pictures to Pray With

- Jesus extending His hand down into a pit to pull you out
- Jesus using a shield to deflect arrows aimed at you
- Jesus coming alongside you to lift a crushing burden from your shoulders
- Jesus gently washing dirt and blood from you after you've gotten beaten up in life

Conversation Starters

- *Practical needs.* When the car won't start, the computer crashes, your dog runs away, or other daily "stuff" happens that you'd usually handle yourself. "My Helper, you want to come alongside me in *all kinds* of trouble. How do You want to help me with _____? And what do You want to do in our relationship as You come alongside me in this?"

- *Emotional needs.* When you feel inadequate for what is required, overwhelmed by responsibilities, depressed by circumstances. "My Rescuer, I feel as if I'm sinking into a pit. Please come and save me! Where should I be looking and what should I be thinking about as I wait for Your salvation?"

- *Relational difficulty.* When you and another person are stuck in feelings of mistreatment, misunderstanding, or other conflict. "Savior, _____ and I need Your salvation. We're struggling with _____ and we can't get through it on our own. Please help us! How are You viewing me in this situation? How are You viewing _____? How would You like to bring help and wholeness to each of us in our conflict?"

- *Struggle with sin.* "Jesus, You came to save me from my sin. You know how I struggle with _____. I've tried everything but can't seem to change. Please deliver me! How can I let You into my need so You can save me?"

Add your own notes:

Summary from Lesson 4, *Knowing the God You Pray To,* by Cynthia Bezek. ©2015, PrayerShop Publishing.

Our King

REMEMBER, THIS STUDY is about talking to God and not just learning about Him. The prayer exercises are as important—or even more important—than answering the study questions.

Are you making your way through the lesson to the prayer suggestions at the end? If you're finding it difficult (and real life can make it very difficult), you may need to look ahead this week and plan the days and times when you'll sit down with God and work through this lesson with Him.

Remember the basic rhythm we're using (open up to God, discover who He is, and respond to Him), and apply it to each of your study sessions. Be sure to begin and end by talking with God. Use the conversation-starters summary throughout the week if you find it helpful.

Suggestions for Pacing the Lesson

Days 1–3: Work through "Discover Who God Is."

Days 4–7: Do the prayer exercises in "Respond to God" and "Continue the Conversation."

I've never lived under the rule of a human king. In my representative democracy, the role of a supreme authority is not only unfamiliar, it's generally considered with suspicion. My sixth-grade social studies teacher taught me that "power corrupts and absolute power corrupts absolutely." In college, my peers wore "Question Authority" buttons.

That slogan often proved to be good advice, as I noticed authority abused time and again on the national and international stage. I was a baby during the Cuban Missile Crisis fomented by dictator Fidel Castro. As a young child, I heard about the suffering and oppression of the Chinese people under Chairman Mao Zedong. Later on it was news of horrific slaughter under the despotic rules of Idi Amin in Uganda and the Khmer Rouge in Cambodia. The abuse of power took less violent forms in my own country. Nevertheless, the Watergate scandal didn't do anything to improve my trust in authority.

I wish I could say I saw the abuse of power at only a national level, but I also saw it in churches, schools, and homes. Through no single person or incident, I became wary—if not downright fearful—of authority.

Maybe that's why the idea of God as King of kings and Lord of lords didn't attract me. My subconscious approach to Him was to keep out of trouble as best I could and hope I wouldn't draw His attention. Being noticed by the King couldn't possibly mean anything good—at least that's what I thought.

Not everyone has my fear and distrust of sovereigns. I have friends who are more likely to think of supreme rulers as far removed from their lives. They won't ever meet such rulers, much less relate with them. If somehow my friends ever did meet a monarch, they might curtsy or bow in respect. If addressed (and only if addressed first!), they might manage a reverential-sounding "Your Royal Highness." But the conversation would be stilted and the discomfort level high.

Other people, schooled in the idea that "we're all equal," shrug off the notion of kings as irrelevant; after all, many monarchs in our modern world are figureheads only. They have no actual power and often command little respect.

No matter our viewpoint, most of us have no idea how to relate to a king, so it is hardly a surprise that when we encounter God as King, we don't easily enter into relational prayer with Him. Yet the image of

God as King occurs often in Scripture. He is called "King of all the earth" (Psalm 47:7), "great King above all gods" (Psalm 95:3), "King of heaven" (Daniel 4:37), and "King of kings and Lord of lords" (1 Timothy 6:15; Revelation 19:16). He's a righteous and gentle King (see Zechariah 9:9); He's the "King of glory" (Psalm 24:8). He is often pictured on His throne in heaven, but we also see Him riding humbly on a colt (see Zechariah 9:9; Matthew 21:5). We're told that He will reign forever (see Revelation 11:15) and that His kingdom will have no end (see Luke 1:33). Even with all this information about Him, you—like me—may still wonder what it means to connect with God as King.

OPEN UP TO GOD

1. As you've been doing each week, begin by inviting God to teach you about Himself. Feel free to borrow or adapt this prayer, or talk to Him with words of your own.

God, I sing songs that exalt You as King. I'd really like to learn to relate to You more personally in that role. You want to be known, and I want to know You. Please help me put aside my preconceived notions so I can know You as You are. Please open my heart and mind to knowing You personally, even intimately, as King.

DISCOVER WHO GOD IS

2. Psalm 72 is a prophetic psalm about the future reign of Christ in His eternal kingdom. Read it and make notes on what you observe about:

    a. The character qualities of the king

Defend, endure, refresh, rule deliver, take pity, save, rescue provide.

b. The quality of life people enjoy under his rule

Great! The people have what they need.

3. Now suppose you live in a country where a king like this rules. I've just moved there, with all my mistrust of authority, and you're responsible for my new-citizen orientation. I tell you about what I learned in sixth grade about the corruption of absolute power, about my college friends' "Question Authority" buttons, and about those myriad news reports of corrupt and despotic rulers, and you quickly discover that those influences have really taken hold of my perceptions.

What would you tell me about your king that might help me? How does he wield absolute power? What are his personality traits? What is it like to serve him?

Cynthia, I can see how you've come to distrust authority, but life here is different from what you're imagining . . .

My King truly cares and loves us as His people. He provides for us. I am blessed to be called one of His.

THE KING'S CLOSEST RELATIONS

A friend recently told me about an account she'd read of various United States presidents. It told of one who, after he took office, discovered that his friends treated him differently. Whereas before they called him casually by his first name, now he was "Mr. President." Their former level of ease and friendly informality was gone.

On the other hand, some of us remember hearing stories and seeing pictures of Caroline and John Kennedy Jr. playing in the Oval Office while their father, President John F. Kennedy, worked. It is said that like other presidents' children, they were always welcome and could be themselves with their president-daddy.

As I pondered these two stories, I was struck by how being "family" changes the dynamic of relationships with people in authority.

4. To get an idea of the difference between a king's subjects and his family, read about Joseph's brothers and about Mephibosheth. In both stories, these people make appearances before powerful rulers—rulers who hold the authority of life and death.

For each account, notice how the standing of the subjects changed when they were welcomed into the family of the ruler. What were their relationships like as mere subjects? What were they like as family?

a. Joseph's brothers (see Genesis 42:1-17; 44:1-5,18; 45:3-20)

b. Mephibosheth (see 2 Samuel 4:4; 9:1-12)

5. Do you see the instantaneous change that took place in the lives of the Bible characters you just read about? One minute they were lowly, powerless, and fearful in the presence of a powerful ruler; the next they were family with privileges.

Romans 8:17 says, "If we are children, then we are heirs—heirs of God and co-heirs with Christ." If God is King, that makes us, His children, members of His royal household.

Revelation 19:6-7 and 21:9 talk about the bride of Christ Jesus, the King. We know from other passages, such as Ephesians 5:22-32, that the church is that bride. What an astonishing truth: We are the bride of the King!

Stop and let those ideas sink in. You're not merely a subject in God's kingdom—you're family! You can live with Him. You are invited to eat, drink, work, and play in His household. He knows you by name, maybe even by a pet name. He loves you! You have privileged access to Him that those not in His family don't have. In order to enjoy your relationship with God as King, it's important to realize not just who He is but also who you are, because He has chosen you to be His family.

In questions 2 and 3, you described what it was like to live and serve in a kingdom like the one described in Psalm 72. Now imagine living in the *household* of a king like the one described in the psalm. What would it be like to live with him as his son, daughter, or spouse? How does being part of his family make you feel? How is life different for you now that you are not merely a subject but a close member of his household?

"When I imagine living in the palace with the king, I see us . . ."

A PRIVILEGED RELATIONSHIP

6. As we continue to explore what it means to be part of the king's family, we'll look at the life of Esther, whose status changed from village girl to queen. How did Esther use the privilege of her position in King Xerxes' household (see Esther 2:5-8,12-14,16-17; 5:1-6; 7:1–8:17)?

7. Because Esther was a favored wife of a king, she was able to intercede for the lives of her people and win their salvation. If that privileged relationship is true even with a pagan and notorious king like Xerxes, think about how God the King might be moved all the more by the intercession of His sons and daughters and bride.

Continue imagining that you are a son or daughter in the household of a king like the one described in Psalm 72. As a well-loved member of the king's royal family, you eat dinner with him every evening. The king is always interested in hearing what is on the hearts and minds of his children and the queen, so he asks about your day. This particular day has been hard. Your heart grieved over the morning news report where you learned about the increasing number of homeless people—including children—in your city. You had lunch with a friend who has been unemployed for ten months now and is becoming seriously depressed. And later in the day you got an e-mail from someone at church telling you that the short-term missions trip you were supposed to go on was canceled due to visa problems with the restricted country you were headed for. It's been a difficult day and your heart is heavy.

   a. Knowing the king as you do—how generous, compassionate, wise, fair, and strong he is—what do you talk to him about? Do you ask him for anything? What?

b. What do you anticipate his response will be?

c. How might intercessory prayer—that is, requests we make to God on behalf of others—be similar to the scenario you just imagined?

CYNTHIA'S DISCOVERY ABOUT TALKING WITH THE KING

Viewing intercession in the context of my close and privileged relationship with God my Father-King is transforming the way I pray for others. It is helping me grasp a bit more fully what Jesus invited us to do when He told us to pray, "Your kingdom come, your will be done on earth as it is in heaven" (Matthew 6:10). The center of my intercession in the past was a list. There's nothing wrong with lists, except that I tended to focus more on getting through my list than on connecting personally with God as I talked with Him about the people and issues that needed His intervention. Sometimes my prayers felt like little more than laundry lists of needs. Or begging. Or wishful thinking.

However, as I am viewing prayer as a way I communicate and build my relationship with my Father-King, intercession is also opening up for me. Less frequently do I race through my list praying, "Please help Maryanne with _____, heal Bob of _____, provide _____ for Blake, deliver Heather from _____, bring revival, show mercy to the homeless." Instead, I am likely to talk with more depth about the two or three people or issues that are especially on my heart that day. Praying for others becomes a conversation with my loving, compassionate King, who cares about the people and issues that concern me.

One day recently, I poured out my heart about Beth (not her real name). I told my Father-King how much I loved her. She was so discouraged, to the point of doubting His care for her and not being able to talk to Him about her troubles. I told Him how much I wanted her to trust Him as the faithful God who would always be there for her. I told Him that I hadn't been able to convince her she could trust Him but I knew He could bring her near somehow. Then I invited Him to respond to me and sat for a while to be still and listen.

God responded in a way that surprised and moved me. Though I don't often think or pray in pictures, an image came to mind. I pictured Jesus leaving heaven, coming to find Beth, leading her back to the throne room, and seating her beside Him on His throne at the right hand of God the King. Jesus talked to our Father-King, telling Him Beth's story in compassionate detail. When He had finished, the King invited both of them to Himself. Jesus lifted Beth in His arms and went over to our Father-King, who embraced them both in His huge, strong arms and whispered something to them. I knew He was answering my prayer.

I was reminded of John 17, where Jesus prays that believers may be in Him as He is in the Father (verse 21). That's what I was seeing—Beth in Jesus, and Jesus and Beth both wrapped up in the arms of the Father-King. Later that week, I heard that Beth had spent a couple of hours pouring her heart out to God and finding His comfort, encouragement, and healing.

My prayers for others aren't always that dramatic, but what does happen is that I feel a sense of release as I give my concern—which I am powerless to do anything about—to the King, who has all power and wisdom and influence and grace and who wants to intervene in the lives of those I talk to Him about. In this way, I can pray from my heart, "Your kingdom come!"

RESPOND TO GOD

Choose two or more of the following exercises and use them as a basis for a conversation with God the King.

PRAYER RESPONSE 1: Knowing the King as He Truly Is

a. Do you have trouble getting close to God the King because of hurtful experiences with human authority or because those authorities have seemed lofty, remote, and uninterested in you? It's only natural that we have trouble trusting an authority who is truly righteous and good when we've experienced a twisted version of that.

Do you experience any of the following when you think of God in His role as King and Ruler of the universe? Mark any that resonate with you.

fear	skepticism
apathy	detachment
avoidance	distance
shyness	pressure to perform
unworthiness	defensiveness
distrust	antagonism
rebellion	wariness
inhibition	hopelessness

b. If you marked anything, talk with God about it. It might be easier for you if you *don't* address Him as King or Lord right now. Instead, consider addressing Him as Shepherd, Father, Friend, or Savior. Tell Him how different the description of Him in Psalm 72 is from how you have perceived Him, even subconsciously. Ask Him to heal any wounds that contributed to your misperceptions and ask Him to give you a more accurate view of the kind of King, Ruler, and Sovereign He really is. Summarize here what you and God talked about.

Misperceptions about God as King

- Corrupt, self-serving, and capricious
- Lofty and distant and therefore uninterested in the "little" things that concern me
- A figurehead with no real power or majesty and doesn't have to be taken seriously
- Someone who is unnecessary because I can manage on my own and don't need to be told what to do

---

PRAYER RESPONSE 2: Knowing Yourself as You Truly Are

It's often difficult to envision ourselves as a loved son or daughter—much less the bride—of God the King. It might feel presumptuous. We might feel unworthy. It might seem too good to be true. We may not even be sure we *want* it to be true! But regardless of our feelings, it *is* true.

If you've entered into a relationship with Jesus, then God calls you family. He is the King. Therefore you are a child—even the bride—of the King, as simple as that. You may *always* approach His throne. You are *always* welcome in His court. He is *always* happy to see you and *always* wants to hear from you.

Learning to accept yourself in your role as God the King's well-loved family member will change the way you pray. It will give you deeper confidence and security. It will enhance your sense of awe and worship. It will protect you from the attacks of the enemy.

a. Read the following passages: Romans 8:14-17; Colossians 3:1-4; Hebrews 2:17; 4:14-16; 1 John 3:1-2. Which one resonates most deeply for you? Personalize or paraphrase it into a prayer you can pray to your King-Father this week.

For example, if you chose the Hebrews verses, you might start your prayer like this: "Papa-King, if Jesus claims me as His sister, then that means I'm your daughter! That helps me understand why it's okay—more than okay—for me to come boldly to Your throne. I don't have to fear that You will turn me away."

My paraphrased prayer:

PRAYER RESPONSE 3: Surrendering to the King

If you tend to resist, or maybe even rebel, against authority—you prefer to be your own boss—then you may already realize that relating to God as King will be difficult for you. But if you want to know God truly and enjoy Him in every aspect of who He is, you will want to address this issue.

Your independent attitude possibly has as much to do with a misperception of God as it does with pride or willfulness. Perhaps things have always seemed to work out better when you've done life on your own. Or maybe you haven't considered what you miss by failing to submit to a truly benevolent and supremely wise authority. Maybe you just have a strong and determined spirit and yielding to anyone goes against your grain. Whatever your block is, are you willing to invite God into it and ask Him to help you so you can enjoy Him for who He is? If so, here's an exercise for talking to Him about it.

a. Start by confessing your feelings about yielding to Him as your ultimate authority. Be completely honest.

b. After you have told Him everything you can think of about how submission to Him feels, invite Him to give you His perspective. Why does He want to be your King—not just to be the King in general but your King *personally*? Still your mind and heart and give Him time to answer. Notice your feelings and thoughts. Do ideas, memories, pictures, verses, words, or phrases come to mind? Pay attention to these; they could be part of God's response.

If you don't seem to hear anything, try speculating on what God might say. If He is truly benevolent and has power to do ultimate good, why might He want to exercise His authority in your life?

c. Respond to what He has said or shown you. Does it help you want to yield to Him? If you need to ask more questions or state more of your reservations, do so. Keep the conversation going as long as necessary.

You may be able to surrender to Him today. If so, do it! But you may need more time. Surrender could be a process that takes place over days or weeks or months. That's okay. What's important is to be *open* to the idea of letting Him be your King. If you can't get there today, He understands. But keep the conversation going. He will help you, and His timing is always right.

Make notes of your conversation here:

PRAYER RESPONSE 4: Bringing Your Requests to the King

a. Think about the people and issues you pray about. For now, concentrate on just the ones that matter deeply to you (not the ones someone has suggested you *should* pray about). It's very possible you feel deeply about these because the Holy Spirit is prompting you to pray about them. Jot these here.

b. Now pick one thing from your list and talk with your King about it conversationally. It may help to picture yourself sitting in the throne room with Him or, if you prefer a more casual setting, strolling in the palace garden. Mention the need, along with your feelings and thoughts about it. Acknowledge God's kingship in relation to the need you've brought up: What aspect of His personality and character corresponds to what is needed for that person or issue? How might God want to reveal Himself in regard to that person or need?

If you need help, remember Psalm 72's description of the king's character. The Holy Spirit may bring to mind other Scriptures about how the King interacts with people.

c. After you have shared your heart about the need and your understanding of God the King's character, invite Him to respond to you.

He may give you a sense of peace about the matter you shared with Him. He may give you an idea you never thought of before—something He may be inviting you to do with Him as a way of answering that prayer. Perhaps He will remind you of a Scripture promise that will make trusting and waiting on Him easier.

Close your time by thanking Him for who He is and for listening to your request and responding to you.

Summarize your conversation here:

CONTINUE THE CONVERSATION

As in previous lessons, feel free to revisit one of the previous prayer responses you didn't have time for or would like to go deeper with, or use the prayer prompts on the following summary pages for ideas on how to start conversations with God your King.

You'll notice that this time I've left blanks in the summaries for you to fill in. This is to get you used to the idea of thinking on your own about new ways to interact with God.

Record your experiences on separate paper or in your journal.

KNOWING THE GOD YOU PRAY TO

Our King
My King . . .

Has welcomed me into His family as His very own child. I have a favored place in His household. He is concerned about the things that concern me and wants me to talk with Him about them. He offers all of who He is—His generosity, fairness, kindness, wisdom, righteousness, power, influence—to bring His kingdom to earth as it is in heaven.

Key Truths About Our King

- He is an utterly *good* king who never abuses authority and always rules in perfect wisdom and righteousness.
- He has adopted me as His very own child and given me all the privileges of being an heir of the king.

Add your own notes:

Praying Throughout the Day

- When you notice people being oppressed, abused, or exploited
- When you hear about enemy threats to what God's kingdom stands for
- When you see poverty

Names to Use in Prayer

- Gentle King (see Zechariah 9:9)
- King of kings (see Revelation 19:16)

Scriptures to Pray

- Psalm 24; Psalm 45; Matthew 6:10; John 16:23-27

Pictures to Pray With

- Sitting with your King at a banquet table
- Strolling in the palace garden with your King
- Watching Jesus ride into battle on a white horse

Conversation Starters

- *Injustice.* "Everything You do is just and fair, Papa King. I am angry about the injustice I see in _____. Would You . . . ?"
- *Acceptance.* "King Jesus, _____ really doesn't understand the invitation You are giving him to be a coheir in your royal family. I can't convince him. But You are able to woo and convince people and help them see who You are. Would You . . . ?"
- *Provision.* "God my King, you own everything and control everything. I have a need for _____."
- *Wise Control.* "Good King, this situation seems out of control: _____. Would you come and rule and reign in it?"
- *Peace.* You are an incredible diplomat, God. I am troubled by the war and disputing I see in _____. Will You please speak peace and bring rest to this turmoil?"

Add your own notes:

Summary from Lesson 5, *Knowing the God You Pray To*, by Cynthia Bezek. © 2015, PrayerShop Publishing

Our Advocate

THIS IS OUR FINAL LESSON! This one will be different from all your previous ones, so let's get started right away. We will be talking about how to cultivate the lifelong joy of discovering God.

Suggestions for Pacing the Lesson

Days 1–4: Work your way through the "Open Up to God" and "Discover Who God Is" steps. As you build your prayer-starters summary, use it to talk to God each day.

Days 5–7: Create the "Respond to God" prayer exercises and finish the prayer starters. Use these to talk to God each day.

Do you remember that in the introduction I told you my goal with this study was to ignite in you a passion to know and relate to God—a passion that makes you look forward to having all of eternity to get to know our amazing, infinite God? If this study has come anywhere close to meeting that goal, then the previous five lessons have helped you realize how incredibly, wonderfully much there is to discover, know, and enjoy about God. To borrow the words of Jesus' close friend John, if it were all written down, "I suppose that even the whole world would not have room for the books that would be written" (21:15).

I want you to continue discovering and relating to God in new ways long after this study is over. That's why this week's study will be a little different. This time, I'll coach you on how to study a facet of

God for yourself, using God our Advocate as an example.

You may think, *Oh, no! Cynthia wants me to do this on my own?* I know it might be a little intimidating. But I'll walk you through the process, and you'll also have the Holy Spirit and your small group as companions on the way. There's no pressure to turn into some kind of Bible scholar or "get it right"; this week is just about becoming comfortable with some tools that will help you continue to discover and enjoy God for the rest of your life. Because I really want you to know how to do this, I've also included the steps from this lesson as an appendix (see Appendix A) so that you'll have them in outline form and can continue to use them for other aspects. (I've included a little more detail there than I provide below, so you can read the appendix if you'd like to see some of the explanations fleshed out a little more.)

Over the past weeks, certain elements have shown up in each lesson. Each lesson has sections called "Open Up to God," "Discover Who God Is," "Respond to God," and "Continue the Conversation." I'd like to show you how you can use these steps to develop your own Bible study and prayer experience around an aspect of God. For this week, we'll use God's role as our Advocate.

STEP 1: OPEN UP TO GOD

I've given you a prayer to pray at the beginning of each lesson. These prayers are simple. Basically you just want to ask God to quiet your mind and heart, open you up to new ways of seeing and knowing Him, and clear away any misconceptions you may have had about Him. Write your prayer here:

God Lord, Thank you for being there for me at any time. Open my heart to receive what it is you have for me. Calm my mind so I can hear you.

STEP 2: DISCOVER WHO GOD IS

The next step we've taken is to look at the Bible to discover who God is. In the previous lessons, I've done all the foundational work for you and then written questions based on what I've learned. In this lesson, I'm going to walk you through how to do that background work for yourself, and then we'll get into the type of questions you may recognize from the past weeks.

A. Orient Yourself to This Aspect

We'll start by getting a basic understanding of the aspect. Sometimes we're studying aspects of God that are pretty familiar, such as Shepherd. At other times, we need to get our minds around the aspect itself so we have a broader understanding when we look at the Scripture. That's certainly the case with our focus this week: Advocate. That's not a word we use all that often, and we may never have encountered a person who fulfills that role for us, so let's do some background work to make sure we understand the role itself.

1. Look up the meaning of the word you've chosen. Look up *advocate* in a dictionary (you can find one online if you don't have one handy). Even if you already have an idea of what the word means, reading a definition often expands your understanding.

2. Brainstorm related words. Brainstorm additional words for this role or aspect to give you a fuller picture and look up those words too. When I think of "Advocate," I connect to words such as *mediator, champion, go-between,* and *intercessor.* I listed those below for you. Please write in their dictionary definitions.

- Advocate: a person who publically supports or recommends a particular cause or policy.
- Champion: person who has defeated or surpassed all rivals in a competition.
- Go-Between: an intermediary or negotiator.

- Mediator: *a person who attempts to make people involved in a conflict come to agreement.*
- Intercessor: *a person who intervenes on behalf of another, especially by prayer.*

3. Think about a human counterpart to this aspect of God.

Next, ask, "How is this type of a person—the human version of the aspect of God I am studying—important?" This step can help flesh out the role for you and give you a tangible example connected to everyday life. Remember, our goal is to *relate* with God in this way, so we need to get a feel for what that relationship might be like.

Why is an advocate important? When might you need a mediator or go-between? Consider circumstances you face at work, tough relationships, times when you have felt steamrolled or ignored, or times you have faced injustice or oppression. Write several possibilities here.

Judge?? Marriage counselor?

As I thought about when I need a human counterpart to this aspect of God, I realized I have an immediate need for an advocate. There's someone in my life with whom I get along just fine. However, we might as well speak two different languages. Communication between us is tough. Sometimes we use the same words but mean different things. Asking questions or trying to clarify often triggers defensiveness on either side, so it's hard to work together. We need an advocate, a mediator, to go between us and help us get on the same page so we can move forward together.

Knowing I was about ready to study this aspect of God, I was excited to realize that Jesus might want to be my Mediator. It hadn't occurred to me that He would step into this difficult relationship with me—I guess I've usually felt all alone when I'm in a dead-end situation like this.

SUM IT UP: Creating Your Prayer-Starters Summary

At the end of each lesson, you have had a section of prayer conversation starters. The purpose of this summary has been to give you a souvenir of your experience of getting to know God and to provide some practical ways to pray according to that aspect.

Now you'll be creating your own prayer-starters summary. At the end of this lesson, you'll find a blank outline titled "Our Advocate." Based on what you have already discovered, begin filling in the category "Names to Use in Prayer." Write in the main names and words for this aspect of God. Start using these names as you talk to Him this week.

B. Explore Scripture

Now that we're oriented to the idea of an advocate, we're ready to discover how God has revealed Himself in this way in His Word.

1. Identify potential Bible passages to study. We need to identify some Bible passages that can help us. There are several ways to do this:

- Ask the Holy Spirit to call to mind Scriptures about this aspect of God.
- Use a concordance to find passages that contain your key words.
- Look up any cross-references in your Bible.
- Explore possible Bible stories that illustrate the aspect.

Because this step can take some time, I've done it for you and listed my raw results starting on page 106, along with the translations that use that particular word. (If you're new to Bible study and would like more information on how I went about finding that list, read the appendix.)

2. Read and meditate on the passages. After you've identified passages that might apply, you have the raw materials to dig in and

"Discover Who God Is" from His Word. Look up each passage below and consider how it might relate to God as an advocate. (If you don't have the translation that is noted, no problem; just be aware that the concept is in the verse.)

Some of the passages will really pop out at you; others won't seem to apply at all. That's fine. Don't think that just because the passage is listed here it must apply. Remember, this is just the raw list of passages that contained the words we were looking at or that had a related concept. I haven't sorted through the list and narrowed it down because I want you to gain experience in doing that step for yourself.

When you do a Bible study from scratch like this, it's to be expected that some of the passages you identify from a concordance or cross-references won't apply to the topic you're studying. It's normal that you'll often hold on to only a handful of passages and put aside the rest. Just feel free to dive in and let God guide you.

a. Read the Bible passages alongside the Holy Spirit. Ask the Holy Spirit to join you as you read each passage, asking Him to highlight what He especially wants you to see and to give you understanding about what they mean when it comes to knowing God as your Advocate.

As you read the passages, note the passages that seem significant and write down what strikes you about each. Leave blanks or write "Doesn't apply" next to the passages that don't connect with what we're doing here.

Intercessor:

Job 16:19-21 *my advocate + witness is in heaven. My intercessor is my friend. He pleads w/ God as one pleads for a friend.*

Isaiah 59:16 (*intercessor* appears in several translations, including AMP) *there was No one to intervene.*

Doesn't apply

John 14:16 (AMP) *The Father gives us a Helper to be with us forever.*

John 14:26 (AMP) *The Holy Spirit is the Helper (The Counselor, Strengthener, Stand by)*

John 15:26

John 16:7

Hebrews 7:25

1 Samuel 2:25

1 Samuel 7:5

1 Kings 13:6

Romans 8:26-27

Advocate:

1 Samuel 24:15 (NLT)

2 Timothy 4:16 (AMP)

1 John 2:1 (*advocate* appears in several translations)

Mediator:

Job 33:23

Galatians 3:19-20

1 Timothy 2:5

Hebrews 9:15

b. "Enter" the Bible Stories. As you read the following stories, place yourself in them. Look for who needs an advocate and who is being an advocate. Imagine yourself in the role of the person needing an advocate. (If you'd like more help on how to do this, read about this step in the appendix.)

Zechariah 3:1-7 (note that "angel of the Lord" often refers to an appearance of God in human form)
Luke 7:36-50
John 8:1-11

The John 8 and Zechariah 3 stories are profoundly touching for me.

When I put myself in the shoes of the accused people, I can feel the heat rising on my face as shame, fear, and hopelessness start to overwhelm me. I feel incredibly alone. I have no defense. I'm doomed. But then God steps in. He speaks on my behalf. And His words have authority! He's greater than my accusers, and His Word goes. I'm stunned. After He dispatches my accusers, He looks at me. At first it's hard to look Him in the eye, but eventually I gain courage, and I am overwhelmed by the love I see there. I'm not alone. Even though I'm guilty, I'm not condemned! If I even considered having an advocate at all, I thought He would only advocate for me when I was innocent. But my Advocate even speaks up for me when I don't deserve a compassionate voice!

SUM IT UP: Add to Your Prayer-Starters Summary

Begin transferring some of your discoveries to the following categories on your prayer-starters summary:

- **Scriptures to Pray.** List the key passages that spoke to you during your study.
- **Pictures to Pray With.** Look at your answer to the question about human counterparts and also think of the Bible stories and characters you studied. Often these will trigger possible pictures for you.

You can continue adding to the different categories throughout the study. As you pray today and later this week, flesh out your prayers by using the names, Scriptures, and pictures you have gathered so far.

C. Pull Together What You're Seeing

Now it's time to pull together the pieces and begin to consider what they mean to your relationship with God.

1. How would you describe God in this aspect? In each lesson, we asked you to describe God to someone else or even to yourself. For example, in lesson 5, you described King to me, imagining that I was someone who distrusted authority and had just moved into the kingdom where the Psalm 72 king ruled. I asked you to do this so you could get a concrete picture and feel for what this personal God of yours is really like. Describing Him as a Person helps us get to know Him that way.

Think of a type of person who might need to know God as Advocate, and then write a description of Him in that role, using the following prompt to get you started.

Person in a difficult situation who would need an Advocate:

"I can see that you need an Advocate. I want to tell you how God is ready to be an Advocate for you. He . . ."

2. What are possible misconceptions about God in this aspect? In each lesson, I've asked you to consider how your views of God may have been incomplete or skewed. I've done that because these misconceptions can interfere with our ability to connect with God as He really is. If we have a negative impression of Him in certain areas, we are not likely to trust Him. We'll hold ourselves back and miss out on enjoying Him in all His goodness, love, and power.

What are some possible misconceptions you or someone else might have about God as Advocate?

When I first started studying this aspect of God, I wasn't sure I had any misconceptions. But as I thought about a real-life situation where I need a mediator (see my story "Think about a Human Counterpart" on page 123) and as I pondered the Bible story that illustrates the role (see my story under "Enter the Bible Stories" on page 126), I realized I had two. If you can't think of any misconceptions, reread my stories and see if they trigger any ideas.

3. What key points stand out to you about God in this aspect of who He is? Now it's time to pull together all the ideas and feelings you've encountered about God as your Advocate. What stands out to you as especially new, interesting, or important?

4. How will this aspect change how you pray and relate with God? Remember that the goal of this study is to know God experientially and relationally, so consider how what you've discovered about this aspect of God will affect how you relate with Him.

How will knowing God as your Advocate change the way you talk with Him? Think through the following prompts:

- Times when I feel as though I need a Person like this
- Something I normally pray about
- How I would pray to God my Advocate about this
- How I could begin turning to God according to this aspect

Remember the person I told you about, with whom I just can't communicate? As soon as I realized that Jesus wanted to mediate, I started praying about this situation with new hope. I've been praying this way only a week, so I can't report any outcomes yet, but I'm encouraged. The other person and I aren't alone in this. Jesus wants to mediate for us.

SUM IT UP: Continue Adding to Your Prayer-Starters Summary

Now that you've pulled together some key thoughts, you're ready to fill in more categories on your prayer-starters summary:

- **My Advocate.** See the description you wrote above, and fill in a description and key characteristics of your Advocate.

• **Key Truths.** Look at your list of key points that stood out to you.

Add these aspects to your conversations with God this week.

STEP 3: RESPOND TO GOD

Toward the end of each lesson, I have asked you to respond to God based on what you have learned about Him in the role you have studied. This is the heart of the study and why we've been doing it in the first place. Our purpose hasn't been to learn information about God; it's been to know who He is so we can talk with Him and relate with Him on an honest, personal level. Knowing God, really *knowing* Him, is the key to both meaningful prayer and satisfying connection with Him.

I've given you prayer exercises to get you started. This time, you'll form your own prayer responses. Here are some of the types of prayers we've done and how we've done them.

• **Address misconceptions.** Often there was a prayer response that addressed the misconceptions about God, asking Him to help us heal from or unlearn the things about Him that were interfering with experiencing Him as He really is.

• **Relate to God according to this role.** Sometimes there was a very straightforward prayer response that gave an opportunity to relate to God in this new aspect. These are simply opportunities to try out a conversation with God in this aspect of who He is. If you were to really buy in to the idea that God is your Advocate and wants to champion you, what would you talk to Him about? What feelings would you share? What questions would you ask?

• **Imagine how your life would change.** Sometimes there was a prayer response that gave an opportunity to talk to

God about what it would be like to relate to Him in this new way—helping us imagine how our lives would change if we asked God to act in this way, if we didn't take matters into our own hands but waited for Him to come through as who He really is. Often this involves both potential risks and benefits, so talking frankly with God about these is a useful part of the prayer process.

- **Receive God in this role.** Sometimes after studying one of God's roles, I realize that I am reluctant, afraid, or even down-right resistant to allowing Him to be God to me in this way. In times past, these feelings would have caused me to avoid God, but now I realize that as long as I leave these areas unaddressed, there will be a barrier between Him and me, and our relationship will be blocked.

  Sometimes these heart issues can be addressed by praying about misconceptions (see above). At other times, confession, repentance, and surrender are required, and that's hard. If that's where you find yourself, God wants to help, so tell Him honestly what your hesitation is about. If you don't know, ask Him. Then ask Him for help and know He will be gracious and patient with you. The key is to open yourself up to Him and ask Him to help you do what you cannot do for yourself.

- **Worship and enjoy God.** If your heart is full of joy over who God is and how He wants to relate to you, your prayer response may be a prayer of praise. Use your own words or look to Scripture (especially Psalms or one of the passages you studied) to borrow words.

- **Intercede.** Discovering God in a new way often opens up meaningful ways to pray for others. A simple prayer such as, *Who do I know, God, who needs to know You in this way?* will open up a rich conversation with Him.

From the list above, choose two prayer-response ideas to help you relate to God as Advocate. As you use them to help you pray, write down what you are doing. Keep in mind that God probably has things to say too, so allow time to listen for His responses. Then reply to what you think you hear Him saying and keep the conversation going. You may either outline and summarize your conversation with God or, if you prefer, write it out.

Prayer Response 1:

Prayer Response 2:

STEP 4: CONTINUE THE CONVERSATION

At the end of each study, we've summed up what we've discovered about God in a section of prayer starters. My hope has been that you will use those summaries to continue talking with God long after the study is done.

SUM IT UP: Complete Your Prayer-Starters Summary

You are almost done with your prayer-starters summary for God as Advocate—only two more categories to go. Fill those in, along with any other ideas you want to add, and enjoy using these new ways of connecting with God throughout the remaining days of this lesson:

- **Praying throughout the Day.** Ask God to help you see where you need Him to be part of your daily life in this role and show you where He would like to be part of your life in this role. Also look back at your answers to the question about how this aspect will change how you pray and relate to God. Then run through your typical day with Him. Or perhaps think of a recent hard day and ask Him how He might like to be more involved on a day like that.

  While I was making lunch just now, my thoughts turned to a friend who is trying to make spiritual progress in a certain area and is facing strong spiritual opposition as a result. As I prayed for him to be strong and to stand firm and not be taken out by the enemy's lies, I realized that my friend has an Advocate, so I asked Jesus to step in and stand between my friend and the accuser. And what do you know? Without even trying, I stumbled onto another way to relate to Jesus as our Advocate!

- **Conversation Starters.** Based on what you just wrote for "Praying throughout the Day," write a few words to start a prayer for each different situation.

Now that you've finished your prayer starters, enjoy a conversation with God. What did you talk to Him about? Record the main points here.

KNOWING THE GOD YOU PRAY TO

Our Advocate
My Advocate . . .

Key Truths about Our Advocate

Praying throughout the Day

Names to Use in Prayer

Mediator
intercessor
go-between
supporter

Scriptures to Pray

Pictures to Pray With

Conversation Starters

Before You Turn the Page

Technically, you have now completed the last lesson of this study. Congratulations! I have a personal word I want to share with you on the next page. But before you go there, please pause a moment and ask God what other aspects of His character He'd like to share with you. Jot down any that come to mind.

Consider doing a study on them, as you just did on "Advocate," so you can continue expanding your conversations with God in days, weeks, and months to come. Who knows—you may even begin a lifelong habit!

Here are a couple of possibilities to get you started:

- Lamb of God
- Great High Priest

Now add some of your own:

Afterword

AS I NEARED THE END of this study, I tried to imagine what God has been feeling as you've been getting to know Him and connecting with Him in these new ways, so I decided to ask Him. If I heard right—and I think I did—God is brimming with happiness. You've received a blessing, but so has He! Here's what I think I heard Him say. If you think I might have heard Him accurately, please take some time to respond to Him.

> My dear child, I've enjoyed these past few weeks more than you can ever know. I've watched you, proud as the proudest father you can imagine, as you took risks and made yourself vulnerable in your relationship with Me. It has brought Me deep joy each time you have opened yourself up to Me in new ways and discovered delights about Me that you didn't know before. You have tasted Me and seen that I am good. How I love that!
>
> Oh, child, there's so much more of Me to know, and it's all good. In Me there is no darkness at all. Now can you begin to understand why I want you to know Me so much? I want to flood your soul with light and life—real life! I yearn to be known, not because I need your admiration and attention but because I am the source of everything good and I long to give Myself to you in ways that will satisfy you.

You've experienced Me. You've enjoyed Me. I've surprised and delighted you. You've felt me tugging at your soul, and your heart has sometimes melted. You responded with wonder and gladness, but your joy can't hold a candle to Mine!

Will you continue going deeper with Me, precious child of Mine? This hasn't been just a Bible study, you know; it's been an invitation to life with Me that is fuller and richer than anything you imagined. Please, please don't stop now. I want to be Your companion now and into your old age and on into eternity. Will you let Me? I love you so much.

How to Explore an Aspect of God

MY GOAL THROUGHOUT all six of the lessons in this study has been to lead you toward the same joy I've had of getting to know God better by discovering Him for myself. I want to equip you in continuing to know and relate to God in new ways without having to rely on a written study like this one.

What follows here is a step-by-step method for studying an aspect of God. I'm using God's role as our Advocate, from lesson 6, as the example here. In fact, what you'll see is, in many ways, a duplicate of the study I led you through in lesson 6. The main difference between that lesson and what you'll see here is that I go into more detail here. I have a twofold goal for doing so:

- First, if you're new to Bible study and would like more help with lesson 6, you can read more explanation and details here.
- Second—and more importantly—I'm hoping that the type of study you did in lesson 6 isn't a onetime experience for you. You can use the same basic steps to study any aspect of God's character. I wanted you to have this study method summarized so that even when this group study is finished, you can keep the following outline on hand and use it to help you discover and relate with more aspects of who God is.

SELECTING AN ASPECT OF GOD TO STUDY

In lesson 6, we used Advocate as the aspect of God to study, and that's the example we'll use here. As you go on to study additional characteristics on your own, obviously the first thing you'll need to do is decide what aspect of God you'd like to know better. The possibilities are vast. In this course, we've been studying His various **roles**—job titles, if you will: Shepherd, Creator, Savior, King, and Advocate. He has many more roles: High Priest, Father, Friend, Brother, Counselor, Bridegroom, Redeemer, Judge, Teacher, and so on.

God also has many **character traits** that, when plumbed, contain rich ways of knowing and connecting with Him. Some of these include: gracious, righteous, faithful, compassionate, joyful, forgiving, holy, and perfect.

Another way of getting to know God is to look at His various **titles.** We often see these in the Hebrew as well as English—titles such as Yahweh Rapha (The God Who Heals), Yahweh Shalom (The Lord Our Peace), Yahweh Nissi (The Lord Our Banner), and Yahweh Jireh (The Lord Who Provides).

God also has many **names** that yield rich treasure when probed. Names like "Emmanuel," "Prince of Peace," "Lord of hosts," "Lamb of God," "Most High," "God of glory," and "I AM."

A study of the **"I Am" statements of Jesus** given in John can be rich. He described Himself as "the bread of life" (6:35,48), "the light of the world" (8:12; 9:5), "the gate" (10:7), "the good shepherd" (10:11-14), "the resurrection and the life" (11:25), "the way and the truth and the life" (14:6), and "the true vine" (15:1).

If you need more ideas, a quick search on the Internet for "names of God" will give you many possibilities.

How do you choose among the myriad options? It's not too hard: Ask God! He knows how He wants to reveal Himself to you at any given time. He also knows what you need to know about Him for your life today and this week. So ask; then listen. Something may come to mind immediately or it may pop up later in the day in conversation, music, radio programs, Bible reading, and so on. When you ask Him for help, He will delight in giving it.

For the rest of this appendix, I'll walk you through the steps that will help you put together a study just like the ones we did for God as our Shepherd, Creator, King, Savior, and Advocate. In fact, the following steps are the ones I used to do my personal studies before I wrote up each lesson for you.

STEP 1: OPEN UP TO GOD

So often we approach a study like this as a learning experience only; even the word *study* puts us into school mode. That's why it's so important to remember you're embarking on a relational experience. God is right with you as you're doing this exploration, so why not do it with Him?

I've given you prayers to pray at the beginning of each lesson. These prayers are simple. Basically you just want to ask Him to quiet your mind and heart, open you up to new ways of seeing and knowing Him, and clear away any misconceptions you may have had about Him in the aspect of Him you'll be studying. Start by praying your own prayer.

STEP 2: DISCOVER WHO GOD IS

A. Orient Yourself to the Aspect

The first step is to do a little work to get a basic understanding of the aspect you're studying.

1. Look up the meaning of the word you've chosen. A standard dictionary is fine. If you have access to a Bible dictionary, you can use that, too. Even if you already have an idea of what the word means, reading a definition often expands your understanding.

Example. When I looked up *advocate*, I discovered that an advocate is one who pleads the cause of another, especially in court, or one who supports or promotes the interests of another.

2. Brainstorm related words. Now consider what other words might be related to this aspect. Knowing a few other terms will give you more places to look in the Bible. For example, you might remember that when we studied "Savior," we also considered "Defender" and "Rescuer." You can list words you think of off the top of your head, see if the dictionary listing gives you any help, and also look in a thesaurus.

Example. When I think of "Advocate," I connect to other words such as "Mediator" and "Go-Between." Those were off the top of my head.

The dictionary definition of *advocate* didn't give me any help, so I'll use a thesaurus to see if there might be more.

In this case, the thesaurus didn't give me much help either! So now I'm going online. I typed "Jesus advocate" into my search engine and found sites that discuss Jesus in this role. I came across an important word I hadn't considered: *intercessor.*

3. Think about a human counterpart to this aspect of God. Consider how this type of person—the human version of the aspect of God you are studying—is important to you. This step can help flesh out the role for you and give you a tangible example connected to everyday life. Remember, our goal is to relate with God in this way, so we need to get a feel for what that relationship might be like.

Example. For "Advocate," I asked myself, *When might I need an advocate or mediator?* Well, if I were in court, I might need an advocate. When I have had an unsolvable dispute with someone, a mediator is a wonderful help. When I feel awkward and unsure and vulnerable in a relationship, a go-between is very helpful. When I'm faced with a situation where I'm not being heard or considered, I need an Advocate on my side.

B. Explore Scripture

Now that we have the words to consider, it's time to find Bible passages that describe God in those ways.

1. Identify passages to study. There are several ways to know where to start.

a. Ask the Holy Spirit to call to mind Scriptures about this aspect of God. If you're new to Scripture and nothing comes to mind, don't worry. Just move on to looking in a concordance.

Example. When I asked for help on this step as I was looking for "Advocate" verses, the Holy Spirit brought to mind two passages: Hebrews 7:25 talks of an intercessor, and Job 16:19-21 includes both advocate and intercessor. That's all I thought of; actually, I was surprised I thought of even those!

b. Use a concordance. I often use one online (search for "concordance" to find a listing and then check out a couple to find one that's easy for you to use). But any concordance should be helpful.

Example. I looked for *intercessor, advocate,* and *go-between.* The online sites often let me search in different Bible translations. Although I didn't think *go-between* would show up in the older Bible versions, it might appear in newer ones such as *The Message* or New Living Translation, so I tried those.

For *intercessor,* the Amplified Bible was pay dirt! *Intercessor* showed up five times there. However, although *go-between* was a nice idea, there were no results, not even in the newest translations. No worries—that happens.

It is often helpful to look up different forms of a word. In this case, *intercede* provided me with four more passages.

c. Look up any cross-references in your Bible. These will often lead you to stories and verses that use similar concepts or phrases.

d. Explore possible Bible stories that illustrate this aspect. You won't always get something for this part of the process, but when you do, it can be very enlightening. Start by asking God to show you: "God, is there a Bible story that illustrates this idea so I can understand You better in this role? Will You remind me of that story, please?"

Example. When I asked God, He showed me an example of "Advocate." He brought to mind John 8, where a sinful woman was brought before the Pharisees and teachers of the law. Although none of the key words are used in this passage, Jesus acted as her Advocate and Mediator.

2. Read and meditate on the passages. Now you have the raw materials you need to dig in.

a. Read the Bible passages alongside the Holy Spirit. The first step is to look up and make notes about the relevant Bible passages from your list. You've likely identified a longer list of passages than you'll actually end up finding useful.

Read each of the passages you identified. Invite the Holy Spirit to join you as you read, asking Him to highlight the parts He especially wants you to see and to give you understanding about what they mean. Some of the passages will really stand out to you; others may not. You might want to hold on to just a handful and put aside the rest.

b. "Enter" the Bible stories. One benefit of a story is that we can imagine ourselves in it and get a feel for what it was like to experience and relate to God in that role. You can ask questions like the ones below about any Bible story to help you enter into the story and experience it for yourself. Sometimes you can put yourself into the place of one of the main characters, or you might imagine yourself as a person in the background.

Example. For the story in John 8, I asked the following questions to imagine I was the woman whose life is in the balance.

- How does it feel to stand in that circle of men? What do I see? Smell? Hear? What's the atmosphere or mood of the group like?
- How do I feel as the Pharisees and teachers of the law pronounce their sentence on me?
- What are my thoughts when they ask Jesus for His opinion? What do I expect Him to say? What do I hope?
- When Jesus goes between me and the men to spare my life, what thoughts and feelings do I have?

C. Pull Together What You Are Seeing

Now that you've explored what the Bible says about this aspect, it's time to pull together the pieces and consider what they mean to your relationship with God. Use what you've seen in Scripture to answer the following questions.

1. How would you describe God in this aspect? In each lesson, I asked you to describe God to someone else or even to yourself. I asked you to do this so that you could get a more concrete feel for what this personal God of yours is really like. Otherwise, our ideas of God too often remain abstract. Describing Him as a real Person helps us get to know Him that way. Think of someone who might need to know God in the role you're studying, and write your description of Him in that role.

For example, in lesson 5, I asked you to describe "king" to me, imagining that I was someone who distrusted authority and had just moved into the kingdom where the Psalm 72 king ruled.

2. What are possible misconceptions about God in this aspect? In each lesson, I asked you to consider how your views of God may have been incomplete or skewed. What are some possible misconceptions you or someone else might have about God in this role?

3. What key points stand out to you about God in this aspect of who He is? By now you have accumulated lots of ideas, facts, and perhaps feelings about God in this role. List the key points that stand out to you. The main points we studied in each lesson came from those I found most meaningful in my personal study. Often these are the points I focused on when I wrote my stories for you.

4. How will this aspect change how you pray and relate with God? Remember that the goal of this study is to know God experientially and relationally, so consider how what you've discovered about this aspect of God will affect how you relate with Him. Write down your thoughts on the following prompts:

Times when I feel like I need a Person like this

Something I normally pray about

How I would pray to God my _____ about this

How I could begin turning to God according to this aspect

STEP 3: RESPOND TO GOD

Toward the end of each lesson, I asked you to respond to God based on what you have learned about Him in the role you have studied. This is the heart of the study and why we've been doing it in the first place. It hasn't been to learn information *about* God, it's been about knowing who He is so we can talk with Him and relate with Him on an honest, personal level. Knowing God, really *knowing* Him, is the key to both meaningful prayer and satisfying connection with Him.

In each lesson, I've given you prayer exercises to get you started. Here are some of the types of prayers we've done and how we've done them. Choose one or more of these to do:

- **Respond by addressing misconceptions.** Often there was a prayer response that addressed the misconceptions about God, asking Him to help us heal from or unlearn the things about Him that were interfering with experiencing Him as He really is. *Example:* In lesson 4, see "Prayer Response 3: Knowing My True Savior."

- **Respond by relating to God according to this role.** Sometimes there was a very straightforward prayer response that gave an opportunity to relate to God in this new aspect. These are simply opportunities to try out a conversation with God in this aspect of who He is. If you were to really buy in to the idea that this is who God wants to be with and for you, what would you talk to Him about? What feelings would you share? What questions would you ask? *Example:* In lesson 2, see "Prayer Response 1: A Sheep Needs a Shepherd."

- **Respond by imagining how your life would change.** Sometimes there was a prayer response that gave an opportunity to talk to God about what it would be like to relate to Him in this new way. We were to imagine how our lives would change if we asked God to act in this way, not taking matters into our own hands but instead waiting for Him to come through as who He really is. Often this involves both potential risks and benefits, so talking frankly with God about these is a useful part of the prayer process. *Example:* In lesson 3, see "Prayer Response 1: 'I am Your creation, in whom You delight.'"

- **Respond by receiving God in this role.** Sometimes after studying one of God's roles, I realize that I am reluctant, afraid, or even downright resistant to allowing Him to be God to me in this way. In times past, these feelings would have caused me to avoid God. But now I realize that as long as I leave these areas unaddressed, there will be a barrier between Him and me, and our relationship will be blocked. Sometimes these heart issues can be addressed by praying about misconceptions (see above). At other times, confession, repentance, and surrender are required, and that's hard. If that's where you find yourself, God wants to help, so tell Him honestly what your hesitation is about. If you don't know, ask Him. Then ask Him for help and know He will be gracious and patient with you. The key is to open yourself up to Him and ask Him to help you do what you cannot do for yourself. *Example:* In lesson 5, see "Prayer Response 3: Surrendering to the King."

- **Respond by worshipping and enjoying God.** If your heart is full of joy over who God is and how He wants to relate to you, your prayer response may be a prayer of praise. Use your own words or look to Scripture (especially Psalms or one of the passages you studied) to borrow words. *Example:* In lesson 4, see "Prayer Response 3: A Song of Salvation."
- **Respond by interceding for others.** Often, discovering God in a new way opens up meaningful ways to pray for others. A simple prayer such as "Who do I know, God, who needs to know You in this way?" will open up a rich conversation with Him. *Example:* In lesson 5, see "Prayer Response 4: Bringing Your Requests to the King."

Using an idea from this list or an idea of your own, pray to God according to this role. Make notes about how you pray, and describe your conversation with God.

STEP 4: CONTINUE THE CONVERSATION

At the end of each lesson, you have had a summary list of prayer starters. The purpose of this summary has been to give you a souvenir of your experience of getting to know God in this new way and to provide some practical tips for how to deepen that relationship.

You can create your own prayer-prompts summary for each aspect of God you study. By doing the steps above, you already have most of the concepts you need. Invite God to join you, and then make lists under the following headings:

> **God My** _____ **Is . . .** See the description you wrote, and fill in a description and key characteristics of your Advocate.

Key Truths I Want to Remember about God in This Role. Look at your list of key points that stood out to you.

Praying throughout the Day. Ask God to help you see where you need Him to be part of your daily life in this role and to show you where He would like to be part of your life in this role. Also look back at what you noted about how this aspect of God will change the way you pray. Then run through your typical day with Him. Or perhaps think of a recent hard day and ask Him how He might like to be more involved on a day like that.

Names to Use in Prayer. Write in the main names and words you studied for this aspect of God.

Scriptures to Pray. List the key passages that really spoke to you during your study.

Pictures to Pray With. Get ideas from the verses you read, Bible stories that demonstrate this trait, and the human counterparts to this role.

Conversation Starters. Look at the list of ways to pray throughout the day and consider how you might involve God in each one. Write a few words to start a prayer for each situation.

Use the summary you've created as a jumping-off point for relating to God in this role.

Now you have the tools you need to begin a lifelong habit of getting to know God and enjoying Him for who He really is. How would you like to continue in this getting-to-know-You process? You could find a friend or two and make a group project out of exploring God's character and talking to Him accordingly. Or you could consider a new aspect of God as a regular part of your life with Him, perhaps discovering a new one once a month. You might even want to prepare a study to share with someone else, such as your prayer group, small group, or Sunday school class. Or maybe you'd like to have a once-a-quarter reunion with the people you did this study with to share the new ways you are getting to know and relate to God.

Whatever you do, please don't stop! There's so much of God to know. As you have realized in the course of this study, the better you know Him, the richer your conversations with Him will be. So keep getting to know Him and keep the conversations going!

Acknowledgments

I HAD JUST BEGUN work on this manuscript when my friend Cindy Polt from Woodland Presbyterian Church in New Orleans asked me if I'd lead a prayer retreat for their women. The retreat was scheduled a mere two months later, and I knew I wouldn't have time to prepare a new retreat *and* write this study. "Would you like to be guinea pigs for the new prayer study I'm writing?" I asked. Bravely, she said they would!

It was a wonderful retreat where God revealed Himself in deeply personal ways to many of the women who attended. I'm so grateful to this wonderful group of women for letting me share the genesis of this book with them. They received with open, honest, humble hearts, and I benefited much from getting to see them interact with God and each other around these ideas.

I am also grateful for the eight small groups and their leaders who volunteered to pilot this study for *Pray!*. They came from all over the country and represented different ages, ethnicities, and denominations and both genders. Each week they test-drove these studies, doing the homework, meeting together to discuss what they were learning, and giving feedback on what worked and what didn't. I took their comments and suggestions seriously. The study you have in your hands is much improved because of their contributions.

About the Author

CYNTHIA HYLE BEZEK is an author, editor, and prayer leader. She lives in Colorado Springs with her two cats and many friends. Widowed in 2008, Cynthia is mother to a wonderful grown son, Ian, with whom she enjoys taking active vacations, usually to Spanish-speaking countries.

Cynthia currently serves as editorial director for Community Bible Study in Colorado Springs. Prior to that, she was worked at NavPress, overseeing their prayer resources and before that, editing *Pray!* magazine.

She is author of *Prayer Begins with Relationship, Prayer and the Word of God,* and *Come Away with Me:* Pray! *Magazine's Guide to Prayer Retreats.*

Cynthia is available to lead prayer retreats that help participants to learn to dialogue with God in two-way conversations, and relate to Him more closely. You can learn more about her and read her blog at http://cynthiaprayblog.wordpress.com.

PRAYER STUDIES

from
Cynthia Hyle Bezek

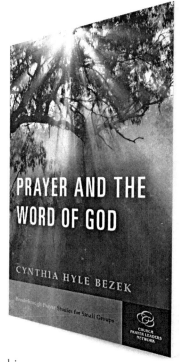

Prayer and the Word of God is a part of a three-book Breakthrough Prayer series by Cynthia. Each six-week study will teach the user something significant about his or her prayer relationship with Jesus Christ. Challenge and equip your small group, Sunday school class or Bible study with these solid, basic truths about prayer.

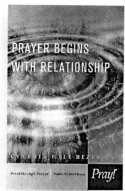

Prayer Begins with Relationship
Prayer and the Word of God
Knowing the God You Pray To

ALL STUDIES ARE AVAILABLE AT PRAYERSHOP.ORG OR THROUGH YOUR LOCAL CHRISTIAN BOOKSTORE.

Quantity discounts are available on *Prayer and the Word of God* and *Knowing the God You Pray To* at **prayershop.org**.

800 217-5200 | 812 238-5504

PRAYERCONNECT

Connecting to the Heart of Christ through Prayer

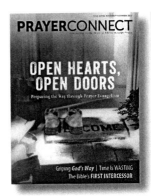

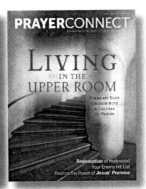

A NEW BIMONTHLY MAGAZINE DESIGNED TO:

Equip prayer leaders and pastors with tools to disciple their congregations.

Connect intercessors with the growing worldwide prayer movement.

Mobilize believers to pray God's purposes for their church, city and the nations.

Each issue of *Prayer Connect* includes:
- Practical articles to equip and inspire your prayer life.
- Helpful prayer tips and proven ideas.
- News of prayer movements around the world.
- Theme articles exploring important prayer topics.
- Connections to prayer resources available online.

Print subscription: $24.99
(includes digital version)

Digital subscription: $19.99

Church Prayer Leaders Network membership: $30 (includes print, digital, and CPLN membership benefits)

Subscribe now.
Order at www.prayerconnect.net or call 800-217-5200.

PRAYERCONNECT *is sponsored by: America's National Prayer Committee, Denominational Prayer Leaders Network and The International Prayer Council.*